PATHWAYS TO THE COSMOS

The alignment of megalithic tombs in Ireland, Britain and Atlantic Europe

Written by Peigín Doyle, with Richard Bradley, Jane Downes, Muiris O'Sullivan, Frank Prendergast, Clive Ruggles, Chris Scarre, Fabio Silva, Clare Tuffy and Ken Williams

PATHWAYS TO THE COSMOS
The alignment of megalithic
tombs in Ireland, Britain and
Atlantic Europe

First published 2020
by Wordwell Ltd,
in association with National
Monuments Service
Unit 9, 78 Furze Road, Sandyford
Industrial Estate, Dublin 18,
Eircode D18 C6V6
T: + 353-1-2933568

www.wordwellbooks.com
ISBN 978-1-9162912-5-6

Text: Peigín Doyle based on presentations by, and
in consultation with:
Richard Bradley,
Jane Downes,
Muiris O'Sullivan,
Frank Prendergast,
Clive Ruggles,
Chris Scarre,
Fabio Silva,
Clare Tuffy,
and Ken Williams
Academic and consulting editor: Gabriel Cooney
Commissioning editor: Una MacConville
Copy-editor: Peigín Doyle
Production editor: Nick Maxwell
Design: Ger Garland
Layout: © Wordwell Ltd.
Printer: Graficas Castuera

Acknowledgements: The publisher would like to
acknowledge the whole-hearted collaboration
offered by the originators of the separate papers to
Peigín Doyle in producing this work, which is
based on their individual contributions to the
PATHWAYS TO THE COSMOS conference held at
Dublin Castle on 15 September 2018 and the
equally generous financial contribution of the
Department of Housing, Local Government and
Heritage toward the book's print costs.

CONTENTS

FOREWORD

I am delighted to have the opportunity of providing a foreword for this publication arising from our National Monuments Service 2018 archaeology conference, organised by *Archaeology Ireland* and in partnership with the Office of Public Works.

Our Pathways to the Cosmos conference held in Dublin Castle that September (a contribution to The European Year of Cultural Heritage—Making Connections), brought together speakers and delegates from across Europe to explore our wonderful shared neolithic heritage.

As our prehistoric forebears sought to bring meaning to their world by constructing places of communal gathering and symbolism, they bequeathed to us a legacy of monumental structures that provides a firm sense of place to communities across Europe.

These ancient monuments have not lost their power or purpose. Communities continue to congregate at these places to celebrate and honour ancient symbology and connections to nature, death and renewal, the power of which still resonates with us today.

We continue to marvel at the engineering skill of our ancestors and the hundreds of thousands of hours expended by communities in constructing these monuments, many built around specific astronomical alignments.

Through gaining a better understanding of the symbology and religion of the tomb builders we gain a fuller understanding of the significance of their tombs, which adds to our appreciation of these important monuments. Recent scientific research on the passage tomb builders of Europe and the exciting discoveries made during the very dry summer of 2018 across the World Heritage landscape of Brú na Bóinne illustrate how steadily over time these monuments reveal their secrets.

Our heritage matters. These panoramic landscapes and their sentinel monuments, many linked closely to the movement of celestial bodies, still inspire our awe. They are prized by communities across the land, rooting our presence in a complex and resilient past. In our guardianship of this heritage, we recognise our obligation to understand, conserve and protect it and to make it accessible to all.

This beautiful publication will help very much to do that. We are extremely grateful to our National Monuments Service, *Archaeology Ireland*, the conference speakers and the Office of Public Works for organising such a fascinating conference, which has been made so accessible through this publication.

We will continue in our mission to highlight the value of our heritage of which we are all

now custodians and will continue to make those connections that are so important for the vitality and well being of us all.

Malcolm Noonan T.D.
Minister of State for Heritage and Electoral Reform

INTRODUCTION

This publication is the outcome of a conference organized for the National Monuments Service, Department of Housing, Local Government and Heritage, by *Archaeology Ireland* and the Office of Public Works and held in Dublin Castle in September 2018. The conference marked a recognition of the importance of the monumental legacy that is a feature of the prehistoric archaeology of northwest Europe in particular and, in that context, it was seen as an appropriate Irish contribution to the European Year of Cultural Heritage, celebrated in 2018.

The particular focus of the conference and of this volume is on the alignment of megalithic tombs in Ireland and Atlantic Europe. This has long been a topic of antiquarian and archaeological interest and research but the framework for interpreting and understanding this phenomenon has changed quite dramatically over time. Up to quite recently there was a considerable emphasis on seeking a level of astronomical precision that perhaps said more about the researchers and our modern western views of time and accuracy than it did about the understanding and beliefs of prehistoric people living in very different cultural contexts. Now it is recognized generally that the construction and alignment of such monuments have to be seen and understood as part of a wider set of cultural and cosmological beliefs.

Taking a step back, the idea for the conference can be traced to an article in *Archaeology Ireland* (Winter 2017) in which Frank Prendergast, Muiris O'Sullivan, Ken Williams and I wrote about the solstitial alignment of passage tombs. Frank Prendergast followed this up with the *Archaeology Ireland Heritage Guide* (82) on *Solar Alignment and the Irish Passage Tomb Tradition*, published with the autumn 2018 issue of the magazine. We were keen to demonstrate that the alignment to the winter solstice sunrise of the very substantial passage tomb at Newgrange was the real deal, as discussed by Ken Williams in a recent paper in *Archaeology Ireland* (Winter 2019). And on the other hand that, while Newgrange is the best-known example of a deliberate solstitial alignment of an Irish passage tomb, it is precisely that; only *one* example of a recurring feature of the Irish passage tomb tradition, that of intentional alignment, which reached its high point in the construction of the tombs of Newgrange, Knowth and Dowth in Brú na Bóinne around 3000 BC.

Every passage tomb in Ireland that can be shown to be deliberately designed in this manner illustrates this phenomenon in a distinctive way. We can think of people in specific locations working actively within, and literally building locally to, a set of wider guiding principles or set of rules. I think the most apt way of describing those principles is in religious or cosmological terms, that is, as a framework that helped people to understand their worlds. And, of course, we know from wider prehistory that there are a number of ways and media in which prehistoric people expressed this regard for the cosmos, particularly the sun. However, as a celebration of European cultural heritage, it seemed appropriate to draw attention to, and discuss, the deliberate alignment of megalithic tombs in Atlantic or western Europe to capture key astronomical events, such as sunrise or sunset at particular times of the year. This also helps to put the alignment of megalithic tombs in Ireland into a wider cultural context.

There are at least 20,000 surviving megalithic tombs in this wider area; monuments that celebrate the lives and beliefs of early farming communities, built from well before 4000 BC down to beyond 2000 BC. The question of their deliberate alignment is an important and relevant topic to discuss in considering prehistoric monumentality and the meaning of those monuments for the people who built them, for research today and for their management, protection and presentation into the future. We are delighted that this theme struck a chord with international colleagues. At the conference and in the papers that followed, leading authorities in the field showed the connections between archaeology and cultural astronomy, linking the material evidence and more intangible aspects such as the cultural ideas, beliefs and ceremonies of Neolithic and Bronze Age societies, with a focus on the landscape and the skyscape.

Thinking of these linkages between material evidence and intangible aspects and going back to the concept of a codified set of rules, Rappaport (1999) and Ross and Davidson (2006) helpfully set out a series of features to help us identify when ritual practices had a religious, cosmological basis. This basis can be identified when the ritual is repeated and linked to specific times and specialized places, reflecting formal or stylized behaviour. People are actively involved in terms of performance by leading actors and participation as the audience. Messages are conveyed that give a sense of the involvement of the supernatural (see discussion in Whitley 2014, 1234). This seems to give a very strong flavour of why such an emphasis was placed on the deliberate alignment of megalithic tombs by people in prehistoric societies, what was involved and why it is appropriate to use the metaphor of those alignments as being 'pathways to the cosmos'.

As you will read in this book, it is an exciting time for the study of this phenomenon given the convergence of the research and interests of archaeologists, astronomers, photographers, artists and others around the idea of alignment being grounded in cosmological conventions and concerns. This convergence is expressed in two UNESCO thematic initiatives on the *Heritage of Religious Interest* (2010) and on *Astronomy and World Heritage* (2016).

A UNESCO International Expert Meeting held in May 2018 in Gran Canaria discussed how these initiatives might best be integrated. The Recommendation (UNESCO 2018) from the meeting stressed that we should think of the sky as the common heritage of humanity, a source of inspiration, respected and held in awe by people across the world now and in the past. It emphasized that understanding the physical laws that govern the cosmos and the abiding human fascination with astronomy and the observation of the sky provides us with the insights necessary to interpret and empathize with how people in very different cultural and historical settings understood the universe. This seems like a good place to start on the path to understanding the alignment of megalithic tombs in western Europe.

Gabriel Cooney

'Everyone feels the urge to get down on their knees and feel the sunlight on their faces as if it were going to feel warm, and we encourage people to do this. As I watch them, I think that the builders of the monuments would be pleased.'

'Each monument is distinct and each sunrise or sunset is different but what is certain is that it is the location in the landscape of the sites that makes the real difference to the light experience.'

'Climbing the hill is difficult, a steep climb in darkness. There is a great sense of pilgrimage in that journey up in the darkness.'

Clare Tuffy, Office of Public Works Ireland.

Newgrange passage tomb at the Brú na Bóinne complex, Co Meath, Ireland.

Chapter 1:

SUNRISE ORIENTATIONS AND THE EUROPEAN MEGALITHIC PHENOMENON

In Europe, our early farming ancestors have left us an amazing legacy of megalithic tombs and standing stones. Furthermore, what has survived to this day is probably far less than the number that they originally erected. In addition to large stone-built monuments, early farmers also created structures of timber and earth.

Megalithic monuments take many forms ranging from standing stones and stone circles to chambered tombs. A chambered tomb is one in which there is an internal space, usually built of stone, to hold the remains of the dead. Such tombs are usually covered by a cairn of stones or a mound of earth. They vary in design and shape. One form, the passage tomb, has an entrance passage that leads from the world outside to the chamber within.

Archaeologists have studied passage tombs from many different angles. One feature that has been noticed is that several tombs, including a number of famous examples, such as Newgrange in Ireland and Maeshowe on Orkney, are built with their passages facing towards the direction of sunrise or sunset at particular times of the year. In some regions of western Europe, only a few tombs seem to follow this alignment. In others, especially in southern Europe, the majority of passage tombs appear to be built facing the rising sun.

ALIGNMENT, ORIENTATION AND AXIS

It is not always clear what direction a monument faces and whether that is accidental or deliberate. Archaeologists use the term alignment if a structure has been directed intentionally towards a chosen point, a 'directed view'. The target point or direction probably has significance or meaning related to the thinking of those who chose the target.

Alignment is often measured by taking a line along the axis of a burial chamber or structure and seeing where it would touch on the horizon or sky if it were extended that far. In passage tombs the view from the burial chamber along or close to the axis of the passage generally forms the alignment.

Orientation is the direction in which a structure faces, such as a point on the compass. It does not mean a deliberate intention to aim at a target point. It might simply be due to the shape of the site and generally has little wider significance.

Even if an alignment towards a particular point can be established, it still does not say exactly *what* the tomb is facing. There are many stars in any section of the sky, many features in the landscape. Still less do we know *why* it faces that direction and how alignment fitted into the overall philosophy of the builders.

Axis is a real or imaginary line around which a body such as a structure or tomb can be arranged in a symmetrical fashion.

Chris Scarre is intrigued by the consistencies and variations in the orientation of passage tombs throughout western Europe, believing that orientation is very important to our understanding of the passage tomb phenomenon as a whole.

One of the first scholars in western Europe to observe that megalithic structures might have been built deliberately to face towards a chosen direction was the English antiquarian William Stukely. Between 1710 and 1725, he studied and recorded many ancient monuments throughout Britain. In the early 1720s, he took a particular interest in the stone circles of Stonehenge and Avebury. He noted

Below: **English antiquarian William Stukeley (1687–1765). (Creative Commons)**

Pages 10-11: **William Stukeley's drawing of Stonehenge in August 1722. He emphasised the importance of measuring and recording sites.**

that the entrance to Stonehenge was oriented to the northeast, the direction of sunrise at the summer solstice. That observation has influenced Stonehenge scholars ever since.

Stukeley believed that the Avebury complex had been built as a serpent-shaped monument symbolizing a primeval divine Trinity. He considered the builders to have been 'Druids' who had developed an earlier form of 'Patriarchal Christianity'.

Above: **Reconstruction of a French Neolithic long house at parc archéologique Asnapio, Villeneuve d'Ascq, Hauts-de-France. (Jiel Beaumadier (http://jiel.b.free.fr))**

Why did the Neolithic peoples of western Europe face their tombs, and their thoughts, towards the life-giving warmth and light of our nearest star? There is no clear answer.

What can be said is that passage tombs and other Neolithic structures have been constructed deliberately so as to face in a particular direction. The direction itself varies across Europe and even within local clusters of tombs. At the regional scale, this intentional orientation, the alignment, is one of the defining features of passage tombs.

Archaeologists have sought to establish if there was any pattern or obvious template in the construction and siting of passage tombs that might explain why their builders did this. If we understand why their builders constructed their tombs as they did, this might tell us something about what our Neolithic ancestors thought about their cosmos, their lives and their societies. It might help us to understand what they were looking towards and the meaning this might have held for them. Was tomb orientation part of a religious belief that spread north from southern Iberia and southern France over time? We do not know if Neolithic societies from the Mediterranean to the Orkneys all shared the same beliefs about the cosmos.

Passage tombs are found widely in western Europe, especially France, Iberia, Britain, Ireland, and northern Europe.

FRANCE

Some of the earliest and most impressive Neolithic mounds in western Europe are found in France. Farming groups migrated from central Europe west into France around 5200 BC. They brought agriculture and stock-keeping with them, largely supplanting the indigenous hunter-gatherer communities. The settlements built by these first farmers of northern France were dominated by the long house, a type of house that they brought with them from central Europe.

Long houses were built of rows of large timbers that supported a pitched roof, with low side walls. They could measure 40m long and seven metres wide. The interior may have been divided into spaces for grain storage, living quarters in the middle and working activities close to the well-lit door area. Up to 30 people could have lived in each house and villages of six or seven

houses are known. In northern France, they tended to face in an east-west direction.

The long house tradition originated in central Europe. In this region the houses faced mainly north-south and orientation only shifted to east-west as the people, and houses, moved northwest towards France. We do not know why they changed direction, whether it was to look back towards the homeland of their farming ancestors or even because of factors such as prevailing winds.

The long houses in France were followed, around 4700 BC–4300 BC, by long mounds,

Above: **The allée couverte at Tressé in the Fôret du Mesnils, Brittany. These long, parallel-sided chamber tombs face in all directions.**

Opposite page: **View of Jacket's Field unchambered long barrow in Kent, UK, taken from the north-western end of the monument looking toward the south-eastern end.**

called Passy-type long mounds, which had a similar shape but were the earliest Neolithic monumental tombs. It is thought they may have been modelled on the design of the long house, the house of the living, and viewed as the house of the dead. They, too, tended to face east-west so there may have been a connection between the long houses and the mounds that came after them. The mounds are found in the southern part of the Paris basin and another small group is found in Normandy.

There was no stone chamber within these burial mounds. Megalithic burial chambers, the first stone tombs, appeared in northwest France.

These first megalithic chambers were followed by the earliest passage tombs around 4200 BC. In a survey of these tombs in the 1960s, Jean L'Helgouac'h noted that most face a point somewhere between east and south. A small group face a point outside that arc but these are all found on the north coast. By contrast, the passage tombs in Normandy, to the east, vary greatly in the directions in which their passages face, so, although some face east, the generally eastward orientation seen in Brittany is not observed.

Another type of tomb, the *allée couverte,* with a long, parallel-sided chamber but no passage, appeared slightly later in Brittany. In contrast to the passage tombs, these *allées couvertes* face in all directions around the compass, showing a change between the earlier and the later tombs in Brittany.

In the region of southern France that lies west of the river Rhone, of 597 tombs surveyed, most face a point between mid-summer and mid-winter sunrise.

In the region east of the Rhone, however, the entrance of the tombs faces west, to sunset, rather than east. The direction of

15

sunrise (or sunset) was evidently still important, but in a different way.

IBERIA, BRITAIN AND IRELAND

In northwest Iberia the earliest tombs date from around 4000 BC. Archaeologist Michael Hoskin surveyed 334 tombs in western Iberia. He found that, looking out from the chamber, 324 of these faced a point between midsummer and mid-winter sunrise.

In Britain, the characteristic Early Neolithic burial mound is the long barrow. These tend to point east-west but not always. There is also a problem of measuring the orientation of the long axis of the mound rather than of the chamber inside. Some British long barrows have a chamber at one end of the mound (sharing the orientation of the long barrow itself) whereas others have chambers opening from the sides of the barrow.

Passage tombs in Ireland face to all points on the compass whereas on the Orkney

While it seems obvious to us now that megalithic monuments in western Europe have an intentional direction of orientation, who first recorded it? Early thinkers on monument alignment were:

WILLIAM STUKELEY 1687–1765
The English antiquarian, doctor and clergyman pioneered the measurement and recording of ancient monuments in England. He published over 20 books on archaeology including *Abury [Avebury]: A Temple of the British Druids* and, in 1740, *Stonehenge*. He realized that the avenue at Stonehenge was oriented on sunrise at summer solstice.

FÉLIX GAILLARD 1813–1900
French hotelier and archaeologist Félix

Below: **The Kerlescan stone alignment at Carnac, Morbihan, Brittany, containing 555 stones, one of several major groups of stone rows in the area. (Myrabella/Wikimedia Commons)**

THINKERS AND THEORIES

Gaillard studied the orientation of dolmens, cromlechs and stone alignments in relation to sunrise and sunset at certain times of the year, particularly those at Carnac in Brittany. He published *L'Astronomie Prehistorique* in 1897, which recorded his studies of six alignments, 225 dolmens and other structures.

SIR NORMAN LOCKYER 1836–1920

The British astronomer and scientist Norman Lockyer was a pioneer of archaeoastronomy. He studied prehistoric monuments in Britain, concentrating at first on Stonehenge but also on megalithic tombs in Cornwall, as well as stone circles and chambered tombs. He found that most of the orientations lined up on May and August sunrise and he concluded that these two sunrise directions marked off quarters of the year. He formed the idea that alignments were related to the significance of certain dates, which he thought were linked to the sun's cycle and the passage of the seasons and, perhaps, to prehistoric festivals. In 1869, he founded the science journal *Nature* as a vehicle to transmit scientific ideas and contributed articles on archaeoastronomy between 1891 and 1908.

JOSEPH PATRICK O'REILLY 1829–1905

This Irish engineer and chemist wrote in 1896 a two-part article published in the *Proceedings of the Royal Irish Academy* on the orientation of some cromlechs in the Dublin region. He also published articles on old Christian churches and tombs in County Dublin.

ALEXANDER THOM 1894–1985

A professor of engineering science, he was interested in the building methods used in megalithic monuments and in the stone circles of the British Isles and France. Based on his measurements, he tried to classify stone circles into different geometrical types. He identified many solar and star alignments at stone circles, though many of these remain contentious. He tried to show that there was a particular interest in certain parts of the solar cycle or seasons, which might have related to a calendar system and to festivals.

MICHAEL HOSKIN

An historian of astronomy in prehistory, Michael Hoskin measured the orientation of some 2,000 European and African megalithic structures. This included hundreds of tombs in Iberia and France. He demonstrated the importance of orientation when considering megalithic monuments.

Below **Bust of the British archaeoastronomer Michael Hoskin at Antequera, Spain, site of the Dolmen de Menga.**

islands, north of Scotland, the entrance passages of Maeshowe-type passage tombs tend to be aligned in directions between southeast and southwest.

CULTURE AND CONNECTIONS

Southern Brittany may have been the source area for many elements of passage tomb culture, which spread along sea routes from there to Britain. The earliest megalithic tombs appeared in northern France around 4600 BC. In northern Iberia the earliest tomb dates are difficult to establish. It is possible, however, that ideas and technology were moving between Brittany and Iberia, perhaps in both directions, and the megalithic tombs spread between the two regions through seaborne contact.

That there were contacts is certain. A green stone, variscite, which was used to make beads and pendants, came from a source at Encinasola in southwest Spain and the beads appear in tombs in southern Brittany, so the

Below left: **Mid-Neolithic necklace of 20 beads of green variscite stone, discovered in 1955 at Bòbila d'en Joca at the town of Montorneè del Vallè in Catalonia. (Museo de Granollers Catalonia)**

Below: **Iberian sources of variscite in the Neolithic and the sea-route to find-sites of variscite artefacts in Brittany. (After Herbaut & Querré 2004)**

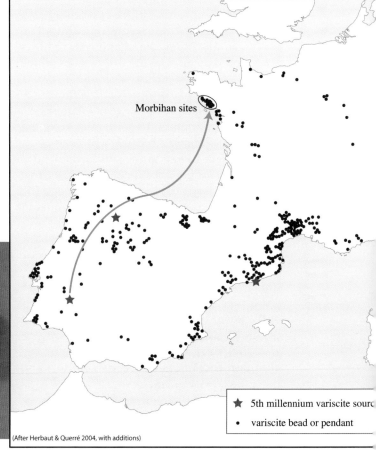

Morbihan sites

(After Herbaut & Querré 2004, with additions)

★ 5th millennium variscite sourc

• variscite bead or pendant

areas were connected. Variscite beads appear also in the graves of the first farmers of northern France, showing that this material was circulating several centuries before the first megalithic tombs were built.

There is evidence also of a shared material culture; megalithic monuments and standing stones are found in both areas, for example, in Brittany and Alentejo in Portugal. Passage tombs in southern Brittany show orientation towards sunrise; so, too, do those in western Iberia.

More than just the structures, particular 'art' or symbols were shared between the two regions, for example, a 'crozier'-shaped motif is found carved on stones in Brittany and also stone settings near Evora in Portugal. So, traditions of tomb orientation and carved symbols may have spread between the two regions as part of wider funerary practices and beliefs about the cosmos.

The regularity of practice found in regions in southwestern Europe suggests shared beliefs and possible connection along western seaways.

From the way in which chambered tombs are oriented throughout western Europe, it is evident that the direction of sunrise was important to these early farming societies. It is obvious that death and the dead were a central focus for thought and ritual.

Highly organized societies with a high level of co-ordination were needed to build structures on this scale. It is possible that construction of tombs drew people from quite far away, through pilgrimage perhaps. Their construction may have unified different family groups in a region into a cohesive wider society.

The direction in which the tomb passages face must have had some meaning for their builders and reflected something of what they believed about their world and what they perceived as other worlds and the relationships between them.

That does not mean that all tombs reflect the same concerns with a target point in the landscape or sky.

Michael Hoskin concluded from his extensive surveys that there was an overall pattern of orientation towards sunrise among megalithic tombs throughout Iberia and south-west, west and northwest France. Along the French Mediterranean coast east of the Rhône, however, they faced towards sunset.

The interest in sunrise orientation may have arisen in earlier centres of monumental building, such as Brittany and western Iberia, but the focus on sunrise weakens as tombs move northward along the Atlantic coast and is much less common in northern France, Britain and Ireland. Overall, the orientation towards sunrise that passage tombs show in Iberia and southern France is lost the further north they go.

Orientation of tombs towards the east may not have been linked in all cases to sunrise, however, though sunrise symbolizes warmth, fertility and rebirth in many cultures. In the case of some tombs, orientations might have been driven by the shape of the land, towards prominent mountains or, perhaps, a harking back to the ancestral home from where the tomb builders had come. Other kinds of symbolism might also have been involved. To draw a parallel with Christian culture, for example, churches tend to face east-west but it is not to face the rising sun.

The passage grave of Newgrange, Ireland,
is aligned southeast to admit the rays of
the rising sun at winter solstice.

A large chambered tomb, called the *Dolmen de Menga* at Antequera, in southern Spain, provides a striking example of the importance of a landform. The tomb is oriented towards north of mid-summer sunrise, further north on the compass than many other tombs. When the surrounding landscape is examined from the entrance of the *Dolmen de Menga,* it is very obvious that the tomb is facing towards a very distinctive-looking mountain that is shaped like the face of a person lying down. The mountain is called today *Peña de los Enamorados,* the Mountain of the Lovers.

Alignment does not mean people were using tombs as observatories or tracking the sun or celestial bodies. Whatever we think is the point of interest in the orientation of monuments, it must have had cosmological or sacred meaning; they were not built or used purely as calendars. Nor can variations in orientation be explained by seasonality and growing cycles.

It may be even that the tombs were not so much concerned with what was visible outside but with something else believed to be happening within the tombs. What occurred within the tombs might have been about death and, perhaps, initiation rites for young people. Passage graves, as homes of the dead, would have been outside the domain of everyday activity and young people may have received sacred knowledge there, or spent time with the ancestors, in rituals that marked their transition into adulthood.

Although there is no uniformity, the similarities between megalithic tombs throughout Atlantic Europe show they are part of interrelated phenomena linked to shared practices, beliefs and cosmology. It is unlikely that this technology and culture developed spontaneously in scattered areas. The connections between regions were not purely trade or technological but based on a shared sense of sacred meaning. The regularity of orientation and practice in southern Europe suggests shared beliefs and possible connection along western seaways.

THE DETECTIVES WHO TRIED TO CRACK THE MYSTERY OF NEOLITHIC TOMBS

In 1764, the French writer the Comte de Caylus (1692–1765), aware of the existence of megalithic tombs in France, the British Isles and Scandinavia, believed they must have been spread via a sea connection by people from the north moving southward and settling along the shores of France in a north to south movement.

In 1899, Swedish archaeologist Oscar Montelius (1843–1921), trying to establish a chronology for Neolithic and Bronze Age development in Europe, thought that megalithic culture came from the Aegean and spread along the north coast of Africa to southwest Europe and then onward to northwest and northern Europe. He maintained the idea of seaward spread of ideas but reversed the direction, seeing it flowing from south to north.

In 1930, anthropologist C Daryll Forde (1902–1973) developed a two-stage theory for the spread of megalithic culture. He noted that variscite beads had travelled north to Brittany from Iberia. From the coastal location of megalithic tombs in Brittany, he suggested that ideas had spread via the sea by people travelling north from Iberia. In the

bers like those in southern Iberia. Overall, he saw a northward movement of people from the south.

Archaeologist Vere Gordon Childe (1892–1957), who excavated the famous Orkney site of Skara Brae, thought that the megalithic collective tombs and the associated cult of the dead were spread deliberately throughout coastal western Europe by 'megalithic missionaries'. He argued that the tombs were not just burial places but also had a religious, sacred meaning for the people who built them and that the links between regions should be understood as a reflection of that.

In the 1970s, radiocarbon dates initially had seemed to show that several centres of megalithic tombs had emerged at similar dates in Denmark, Brittany and southern and southwestern Iberia and perhaps Ireland too.

second stage, these people and ideas had spread by sea onward through the Irish Sea to Scotland and Ireland. He saw a connection in that chambered cairns in Brittany and in northern Scotland have corbel-vaulted cham-

Above: **Dolmen de Menga, a chambered tomb at Antequera, Spain, which is not aligned on the sun but on a nearby mountain.**

Right: **Peña de Los Enamorados mountain in southern Spain, shaped like a human face lying down. The Dolmen de Menga is aligned on the mountain.**

Opposite page: **Pawton Quoit megalithic tomb, Cornwall, one of many studied by British archaeoastronomer Sir Norman Lockyer. (Alan Simkins)**

This helped give rise to the idea of a process of parallel development at different locations in the Neolithic.

However, later, improved radiocarbon dating showed that tombs in some areas were earlier than others, for example, they are earlier in Brittany than in Britain, Ireland and northern Europe. They also might be earlier than those in Iberia, though there is evidence suggesting an early origin of megalithic standing stones and, perhaps, simple tomb chambers in western Iberia.

WHAT WE THINK NOW

Based on these improved chronologies, as well as new data from advances in DNA, isotope analysis and new archaeological excavations, the latest view has come back to the idea that tomb technology and culture spread along the western seaways, with connections between Iberia and Brittany and northern France and Britain.

●

Adapted by Peigín Doyle from the conference presentation by Professor Chris Scarre.

Megalithic passage tombs began to
be built in Iberia around 4000 BC.

Chapter 2:

THROUGH A GLASS DARKLY: ORIENTATION UNCERTAINTY, PASSAGES AND STARS IN THE WESTERN IBERIAN TRADITION

Megalithic passage graves in Iberia were built over a period of 500 years between 4000 BC and 3500 BC, though they continued to bc uscd until the Early Bronze Age. Over 2000 passage tombs are identified in national records of monuments in Portugal. However, of this number, only 762 are still known or can be identified.

Archaeologist Fabio Silva has led a seven-year survey of surviving passage tombs in Portugal and Galicia.

Passage tombs first appeared approximately 1500 years after the first agricultural society developed in Iberia. Pastoral society developed in Iberia around 5600 BC, which was 1500 years before the UK and Ireland.

Agriculture and pastoralism had emerged first in the Middle East and spread through Europe, moving very quickly along the western Mediterranean coast. It is very likely that Neolithic pastoralists spread via the sea and settled in places that had not been occupied by existing Mesolithic hunter-gatherers. This Neolithic society slowly spread throughout the country, starting from the south, potentially intermixing with the earlier indigenous population.

These pioneers were not farmers in the modern sense. In the north of the country, their agriculture was more like garden growing or horticulture combined with pastoralism. They domesticated sheep and goats, made polished stone tools and produced the first pottery in Iberia.

A series of mountain ranges separated by many river valleys forms the landscape of northwestern Iberia. The Neolithic people of northern Portugal, who sourced their food from cultivation, gathering and hunting, are believed to have followed a seasonal subsistence mode of living, moving to the mountains in summer to pasture their animals and find food for themselves. In winter they would have moved back down to the sheltered river valleys.

Around 4000 BC, megalithic monuments started to appear in Iberia, particularly in the north. They were mainly passage tomb types ranging from very small, low structures to more developed versions with much larger chambers, a passage, a large covering cairn and a forecourt. The forecourt was never straight but always asymmetrical or angled to one side, though not always to the same side. They are similar to passage tombs in Ireland but those in Iberia are typically not as big.

PRIOR SURVEY

Astronomer Michael Hoskin, who was a pioneer of archaeoastronomy, from the 1980s surveyed about 2000 megalithic structures across the western Mediterranean, including in northwest Iberia. With a compass he measured the axis of structures to determine what way they faced, trying to establish if any patterns in alignment or orientation could be seen.

Having found no single pattern in the orientation of the tombs of northwest Iberia,

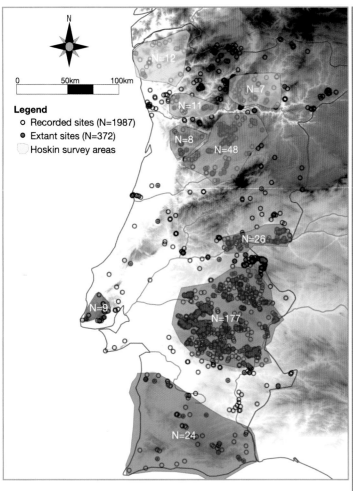

Legend
o Recorded sites (N=1987)
● Extant sites (N=372)
Hoskin survey areas

N=12
N=7
N=11
N=8
N=48
N=26
N=9
N=177
N=24

Left: Recorded and surviving megalithic sites in western Iberia with the location of sites surveyed in the 1980s by archaeoastronomer Michael Hoskin highlighted. (Fabio Silva)

Opposite page above: A survey of surviving passage tombs requires a consistent method for establishing their orientation. (Fabio Silva)

Opposite page below: The point on a tomb's structure from which measurements are taken will determine where on the horizon the tomb seems to be oriented. (Fabio Silva)

the autumn and winter. Modern thinking differs from this view.

Hoskin surveyed and compared monuments over wide geographic areas. However, prehistoric communities were small. Their typical monuments were found in small clusters and were not spread across thousands of kilometres. If clusters from different regions are bundled and analyzed over wide distances, small, localized patterns of orientation will be lost. A typical cluster in the Mondego river valley held 10 to 12 structures. When measurements are compared at the scale of these localized clusters, patterns of orientation in prehistoric tombs are found. That is the finding of the current survey of surviving passage tombs in Portugal and Galicia.

This survey sample comprised around 400 passage tombs that excavation reports or other information had shown to have enough of a surviving structure to be able to indicate a clear orientation. The survey has been going on for seven years and has covered nearly 95 per cent of the identified passage tombs in the north of Portugal. One hundred and thirty-one passage tombs in Portugal,

Hoskin suggested that they were aligned to sunrise or sun climb on the day when people first started building them. Sun climb is how the sun climbs across the sky after it has risen. In this way he explained why they had different orientations, because their construction would have begun on different days in

mostly in the north, and 37 in Galicia, have been examined. Of these, only 104 are complex enough to present a passage; the rest are small and simpler containing only a megalithic chamber with an entrance. The survey is starting now to move into the south.

THE WINDOW OF VISIBILITY APPROACH

How can you tell what way a passage tomb is facing? Do you stand at the entrance and look out? What happens if mountains or trees get in the way?

To conduct any kind of survey, you have to make certain assumptions and use standard operating methods to get consistent results. To measure an orientation, you have to take a set point in the structure, extend a line from that point and see where it points towards on the horizon. If tombs are different in size and state of repair, how do you ensure you are measuring the same thing, from the same position, each time? Passage tombs in north-west Iberia were not built along straight, centred lines.

It has to be decided from what point in the passage tomb you take a line and extend it to the horizon. Do you do it from the centre of the entrance, the centre of the passage, the middle of the chamber or from the sides? Depending on where you stand in order to extend a line, you may end up with very different orientations, as much as 20–30 degrees different. More importantly, how do you know that you are capturing the orientation of the monument as it would have been understood by the prehistoric people who built it? Getting this wrong means that the surveyor may miss the very thing that the Neolithic builders were interested in.

The Iberian survey used an innovative methodology. Using the chamber as the viewing location, it started by taking the minimum possible line of sight between the inside of the chamber and the horizon outside and then the maximum possible line of sight from the inside of the chamber. That produced a 'viewing window', which was called 'the maximum window of visibility'. This is slightly wider than the window from any one

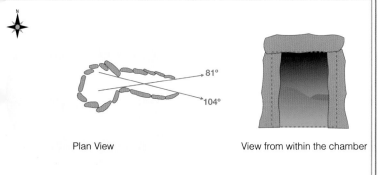

Plan View   View from within the chamber

81°

104°

Mars and the Milky Way over modern Iberia.
Surveyors used computer programmes to
reconstruct the Neolithic horizon.

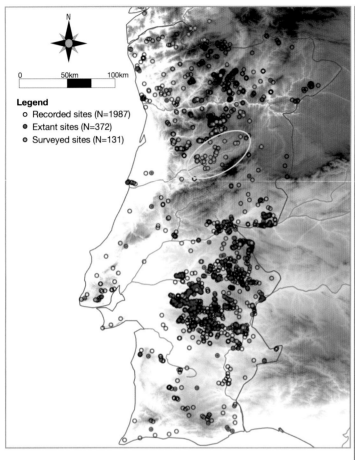

Legend
○ Recorded sites (N=1987)
● Extant sites (N=372)
◓ Surveyed sites (N=131)

of the same period that were related geographically, architecturally and with similar archaeological finds. Windows then were compared between them, under the assumption that, if any patterns are to be found, it is at the community scale, rather than at much larger regional and national scales. If an overlap in all their windows existed then that is the region of the sky where one can say they were all intentionally oriented towards and, therefore, where one should look for celestial objects.

RECONSTRUCTING THE NEOLITHIC HORIZON

To measure the location of a body in the sky, it is necessary to see the horizon and the altitude of the celestial body in the sky. If a mountain blocks the view of the sun at sunrise, then the sun has to rise higher in the sky to climb over the mountain before it is seen. By the time it has done that, it is already further south than it would be if it were rising on a flat horizon.

No one knows how high vegetation grew in the Neolithic and large-scale forestry planting has taken place in modern Portugal, often blocking the view of the horizon.

To remove the effect of these obstacles, the surveyors used GIS and digital elevation models to reconstruct the Neolithic horizon. Over that they laid the window of maximum visibility, to show what would have been visible from inside the chamber. Because it was a digital exercise it was possible to plot the orbit of celestial bodies as they happened in the Neolithic and to try to find a match for the orientation of the tomb.

point inside the chamber but includes all possible viewing windows in its span. If a passage tomb was pointing to a body in the sky, that body would have to be visible inside the frame created by that window.

To check whether patterns of orientation existed, the surveyors picked tombs that independent evidence had shown belonged to the same identifiable cluster, that is, monuments

MOUNTAIN RANGE OF THE STAR

In the Mondego valley, seven passage tombs were surveyed that were already known to be oriented towards a mountain range on the horizon called *Serra da Estrela*. It is believed the ancient people spent their summers in those mountains, indicating a connection between the passage tombs in the river valley, where they wintered, and their living space in the summer. The pattern of this cluster lines up not with the highest point but with a relatively flat area of the mountain range.

Checking this region of the horizon for a solar orientation, the sun would have risen in that space in early February or late October,

---

Below: **In the Neolithic, Aldebaran rose before sunrise in early May at the place above the Serra da Estrela mountains towards which passage tombs were facing. (Fabio Silva)**

Opposite page: **Sites surveyed in the Mondego valley are within the yellow circle. (Fabio Silva)**

PAINTED TOMBS

Passage tombs in northwest Iberia were lavishly painted. In the best surviving example, *Dolmen de Angela's, Oliveira de Frades,* Portugal, every stone in the chamber has preserved paint, the prehistoric decorators having used colours of ochre red, black, white and gold. Some other tombs were decorated also with stone carvings.

which would have been either too cold or too late in the year to have been used as a calendar date to start migration.

However, 6000 years ago, the star Aldebaran also rose there. Aldebaran is the eye of the bull in the Greek constellation of Taurus, is coloured red and is the fourteenth brightest star in the night sky. Moreover, it would have been first visible above the mountains at the place where the passage tombs were facing in late April to early May. Aldebaran would have risen in the sky before sunrise, the last star to rise before the sun's rays blot it out — a morning star. The rising of Aldebaran above the point on the mountains might have been used as a calendar notice to start migration in early May.

Each day Aldebaran would have risen four minutes earlier and so would have climbed higher in the sky until it touched the western horizon for the first time in mid-September. This would have happened over the river valley where the passage graves sat. So, the seasonal migration up and down those mountains might have been triggered or heralded by the movements of this star in the sky.

In Portuguese, *Serra da Estrela* means Mountain Range of the Star.

Three other passage tomb clusters are known between the Mondego and the Douro valleys. The methodology was tested on the most developed tombs in those clusters. In all cases a pattern was found. Furthermore, when smaller tombs without a passage were checked, their entrances followed the overall pattern of the cluster they belonged to. But these patterns were not always the same as that found in the Mondego valley.

Two clusters seem to be targeting Aldebaran. Two other clusters seem to be focusing on the same region of the sky but on a different star. It might be Elnath, another star in the Taurus constellation, on the tip of the bull's horn. Elnath is white-bluish and not as bright as Aldebaran. Alternatively, it might have been focused on another bright red star, in the constellation Scorpius, called Antares. Antares is on the opposite side of the sky to Aldebaran so when Aldebaran was rising, Antares was setting, in a dance of opposites or perhaps complementarity.

Having identified these patterns of orientation on Aldebaran and possibly Elnath/Antares, they were checked for other tombs that do not belong to any known cluster. The results to date have shown that 99 tombs out of 104 surveyed appear to be oriented towards one or other of just three stars — Aldebaran, Elnath or Antares and a third, Alnilam, one of the stars in Orion's Belt in the Orion constellation. Throughout Galicia and Portugal, Aldebaran is a match for 70 per cent of the passage tombs tested.

Archaeoastronomy is not the study of astronomy as practised by ancient societies. Rather, it seeks to understand people's cultural and symbolic perceptions of phenomena in the sky. It examines how people in the past 'have understood the phenomena in the sky, how they used phenomena in the sky, and what role the sky played in their cultures'.

Opposite page: **The blue Pleiades star cluster (left) and Hyades cluster (right) close to yellow Aldebaran. Neolithic people were not solely concerned with movements of the sun. (NASA/Rogelio Bernal Andreo)**

Many archaeologists think that using the concept of astronomy can colour archaeological interpretation of how and why prehistoric structures are aligned. The term astronomy suggests using specially-built observatories to make scientifically-inspired observations of the skies. This might lead archaeologists to assume that tombs were oriented in a particular direction to be used as observatories because the builders had a scientific curiosity about some aspect or movement of celestial bodies.

Astronomy can bring also a tendency to only consider the sun in the orientation of passage tombs, perhaps because modern western societies, with their light pollution and city buildings, have lost contact with the stars and the moon. However, historic and ethnographic records suggest that the moon and the stars played a role too in ancient people's skyscapes. For archaeologists this means that the orientation of a structure towards where the sun rises or

FROM ASTRONOMY TO SKYSCAPE

sets does not automatically mean that ancient people were focused on the sun, because other celestial objects rise and set in the same part of the sky.

Rather than think in terms of astronomy, archaeologists have begun to adopt the term 'skyscape', which stands for what people see when they look at the sky; what stories they tell, what gods and mythological figures they see, what fears, motivations and meanings they attach to the celestial objects. Skyscapes free up researchers to consider a wider framework of research methodologies as well as culturally-rooted interpretations and interests in the sky and the celestial objects. After all, most societies see the world in a more magical, rather than scientific, way and this likely would have been equally true of prehistoric societies.

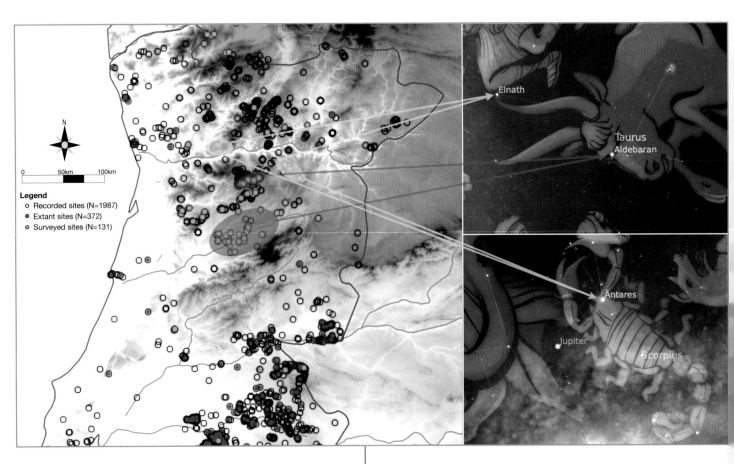

Five other passage tombs surveyed could not be explained by any celestial orientation. They did not face sunrise, moonrise or any bright star, which means that something else might have happened.

Overall, Michael Hoskin's conclusion that there was no pattern is upended when tombs are examined at the level of small clusters using the maximum window of visibility approach. Very strong patterns were found, which suggest the stars might have had a possible function for those communities but we do not know what it was. In this particular area of Europe, the best explanation for alignments on stars is that they might have served as seasonal markers for the builder communities. However, people did not need to see the

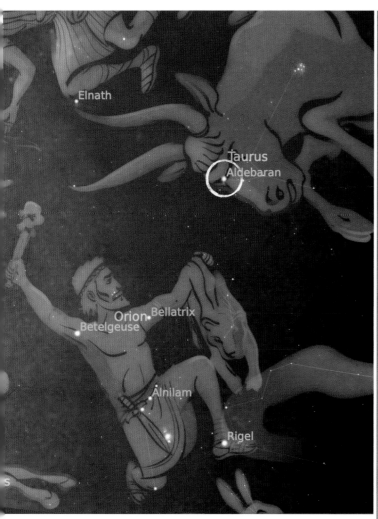

must know already that this is where the star will rise. The knowledge comes before the tomb. So why build the tomb?

It reminds us that even when we can establish a point on which a passage tomb seems to be focused, we still cannot be sure what it meant in the minds of the tomb builders. We cannot know how the ancient people used their tombs, or even if they did look out on the horizon at all and, if so, from what point within the tomb.

We need to think about the world as it was conceived by the Neolithic people and to look at other aspects of material culture and archaeology for possible insight. One theory is that, as well as potentially holding human remains, the tombs might have been used for rites of passage for young people who qualified as adults by spending time in the tombs with the bones of their ancestors. Within the tomb they might have been given secret knowledge that was considered sacred to make them part of adult society. It might have been possible from within the tomb to observe the rising of a significant star at dawn or to see it rise inside the chamber a few days before it became visible to people outside. This could have been part of that 'secret' knowledge imparted unto them at the culmination of the rite of passage.

Future work will continue not only to survey more passage tombs but also to explore this issue of stellar visibility from inside these monuments.

●

Adapted by Peigín Doyle from the conference presentation by Dr Fabio Silva.

star rise to know when it was time to move back down from the mountains for the winter.

The paradox is that, in order to orient a passage tomb, you need to know already that there is an object of interest or a pattern of movement in the sky. To build a passage tomb to observe the rise of Aldebaran, you

Chapter 3:

A COSMOLOGICAL INTERPRETATION OF THE ALIGNMENTS OF NEOLITHIC BURIAL MONUMENTS IN ORKNEY

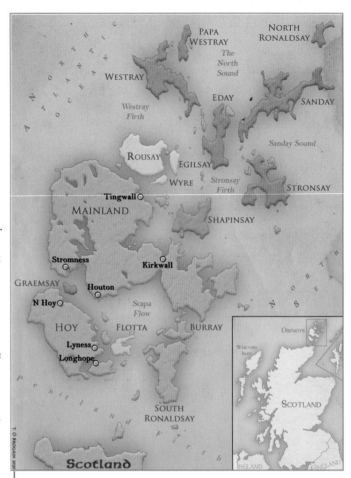

O n the Scottish islands of Orkney, 59 degrees north of the equator, there are great contrasts in light and darkness in the days and across the seasons. In winter the shortest day sees about six hours of daylight and in summer this lengthens to 18 hours.

Orkney has a wealth of prehistoric sites especially from the Neolithic period. The great Orkney sites such as Skara Brae Neolithic village, the Ring of Brodgar stone circle, Maeshowe passage tomb and the Stones of Stenness were built almost 1000 years before Stonehenge and have World Heritage status.

Archaeologist Jane Downes has studied the relationship between the Neolithic monuments of Orkney and the sun, the landscape and the skyscape in which they are set. She has discovered that the Neolithic builders oriented their burial monuments in relation to the sun, pressing into service the sea, mountains, landscape and architecture to draw in the light. They also manipulated access to that light, blocking it off or allowing it through.

ORKNEY SOCIETY

There is evidence of settlement in the Orkney islands from Mesolithic times or Middle Stone Age onwards. In the Mesolithic, Stronsay had an established, though partly seasonal, population while Orkney was well populated throughout the Neolithic or New Stone Age with estimates of a population of 10,000 or more. In the Early Neolithic, c. 3800–3300 cal. BC, people lived in large houses, which sometimes occurred in pairs,

Above: **The islands of Orkney northeast of Scotland.**

Orkney's Neolithic monuments are oriented in relation to the sun. Midwinter sunset shines across the Hoy hills towards Maeshowe passage tomb.

The way in which a tomb passageway or lightbox must face if the chamber is to be flooded by sunlight is decided by the time of year and the time of day. At the autumn and spring equinoxes the sun rises in the east and sets in the west. At the midwinter solstice, the sun rises in the southeast and sets in the southwest. At the summer solstice, it rises in the northeast and sets in the northwest.

To face the rising sun at midwinter solstice, a tomb must be oriented southeast and to catch the setting sun's rays at midwinter it must face southwest. At midsummer sunrise, it must face northeast and for sunset it must turn to the northwest.

Tombs oriented to the south are aligned with the sun's rays at noon while tombs oriented to the north are so situated that solar alignment is prevented completely.

The entrance passages of Orkney Maeshowe-type passage tombs are all aligned either east, west, south or between these directions. They tend to align mainly to directions between southwest and southeast, that is, towards the sun at winter solstice.

and burial cairns were stalled, or Orkney Cromarty-type, tombs. In the Later Neolithic, c. 3300–2500 cal. BC, there were villages and passage graves, or Maeshowe-type, tombs. In the Bronze Age the mode of settlement changed to more dispersed settlement of single or double houses, and burial form changed to cists and earthen burial mounds or barrows.

Above: **The entrance passage of Maeshowe tomb draws in the light of winter solstice sunset. (© Charles Tait)**

Right: **The Ness of Brodgar, looking northeast towards the Stones of Stennes with excavation site in the foreground. (Hugo Anderson-Whymark)**

Opposite page: **The Ring of Brodgar stone circle. The entrances are aligned to midwinter sunrise and midsummer sunset. (Historic Environment Scotland)**

RING OF BRODGAR AND NESS OF BRODGAR

Brodgar is a very narrow finger of land separating two lochs, Harray and Stenness, in the West Mainland area of Orkney.

The Brodgar isthmus is aligned naturally northwest to southeast. This natural alignment may have been viewed as auspicious, describing a sacred alignment and perhaps an ancient route way.

At the tip of the isthmus is the significant Neolithic site of the Ness of Brodgar. Within the Ness of Brodgar are several stone structures built on a massive scale. The most notable, Structure 10, is one of the largest Neolithic stone buildings in Britain, with outer walls four metres thick. It was built around 3000 BC. Inside is a cross-shaped chamber, similar to the central chamber at Maeshowe passage tomb.

It is believed to have been the last major monument to be built on the Ness of Brodgar site. In the last phases of activity, around 2450 cal. BC, hundreds of cattle were slaughtered and eaten in a great feast and piles of cattle shinbones were placed in the building's passageway. Structure 10 was discovered in

The central chamber of Maeshowe passage grave, the largest passage tomb in Orkney.

2008 along with the remains of hundreds of cattle leg bones and some red deer.

There are two stone circles, the Ring of Brodgar and, across the very narrow channel between the two lochs, the Stones of Stenness. Roughly equal distance from both Stenness and Maeshowe is the Neolithic settlement of Barnhouse.

The Ring of Brodgar stone circle and henge has two entrances; the southeastern entrance is aligned towards midwinter sunrise and the entrance on the northwest faces towards mid-summer sunset.

An enormous wall, still visible as a landscape feature, stretches across the width of the Brodgar peninsula, possibly blocking or controlling access to the Ring of Brodgar and Ness of Brodgar. It may have acted as a boundary between the ritual, sacred area and the rest of the landscape and controlled access, both physical and spiritual, to the area.

MAESHOWE

The Late Neolithic passage tomb of Maeshowe is the largest passage tomb in Orkney, covered by a mound 35m in diameter and 7.3m high. It has a large central chamber and three sub-chambers reached through a long, low entrance passage. In sophistication of design and construction it is often compared to Newgrange in Ireland's Boyne valley, although Newgrange is aligned to the midwinter rising sun, not to sunset.

It has been estimated that up to 100,000 labour hours would have been required to build Maeshowe. Despite this extraordinary effort, no human remains or grave goods were found in it. Later, between the ninth

Setting sunlight strikes the
rear wall and chamber in
Maeshowe on the days
around the winter solstice.

42

The light of midwinter sunrise pours down the lower passage of Taversoe Tuick having first hit the sea and been reflected up.

The two-storey passage grave of Taversoe Tuick, Rousay, seen from the north.

and 12th centuries AD, it was opened and re-used by Vikings who left a large number of runic inscriptions on the chamber walls.

Maeshowe faces to the southwest and at the midwinter sunset the sun's rays enter and stream down its passage to hit the back wall. This happens for some days either side of the winter solstice.

Maeshowe has a relationship not just with the sun but with the Orkney landscape. The island of Hoy is the highest point in the whole of Orkney. The sunlight enters the chamber only when the sun appears at a certain angle over the Hoy hills and shines over the Barnhouse standing stone to enter the tomb. The hills frame the sun as it shines down the passageway.

Another exceptional feature is the installation of a triangular-shaped stone set into a cavity in the passage, which can be moved at will. This stone could be swivelled to block

---

Above: **The entrance to the upper tomb of Taversoe Tuick, which faces north. (Historic Environment Scotland)**

the passage at the appropriate moment, shutting off the entry of light along the passage. A slight gap left at the top allows a small amount of light to enter. Each of the three chambers also had a small, triangular blocking stone at the entrance that could partially close the hole. These acted as a mechanism for controlling or manipulating the access of sunlight. The stones now lie on the ground in front of their chambers.

Underneath the passage that draws in the sunlight there is a substantial stone-lined drain, a feature that has been found in some other Orkney tombs.

TAVERSOE TUICK

The island of Rousay is famed for the 14 Neolithic tombs and other archaeological sites it holds. One tomb, Taversoe Tuick, is remarkable for its two-storey design. It is a rare form of tomb and is one of only two such tombs known on Orkney.

The two storeys of Taversoe Tuick tomb are built one directly above the other and the two levels are separated by a stone floor that prevented access from one to the other.

The tomb is built on a hill so each passage is at ground level, one on the uphill slope and the other on the down side. The lower chamber is below ground and five vertical stones divide it into four compartments opening from the central space. Its main axis is at right angles to the passage. On the lower level a long passageway and drain lead to and from the chamber, which faces towards the winter solstice sunrise. Although it faces more due south than southeast, the sun's rays are reflected up from the sea into the tomb, shine

Above: **The Crantit tomb and its cists. (Beverley Ballin Smith)**

Below: **The location of the lightbox at the roof slabs of Crantit tomb. (Beverley Ballin Smith)**

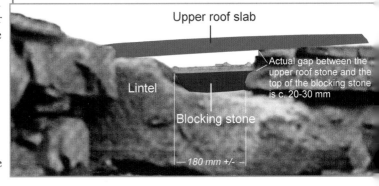

Upper roof slab

Actual gap between the upper roof stone and the top of the blocking stone is c. 20-30 mm

Lintel

Blocking stone

— 180 mm +/- —

along the passageway and hit the back wall of the chamber. They then shine higher up and illuminate more of the passageway. The builders knew the sea enhanced the sunlight and used that fact in building and orienting the tomb.

When first discovered, several skeletons and cremated human bone were found. The other finds included two Unstan bowls, a mace-head, flint arrowhead and scrapers and 35 disc-shaped beads of grey shale. The passage had been blocked off.

The entrance passage to the upper chamber faces north so it can never be lit by the sun.

CRANTIT

The Crantit tomb on mainland Orkney was dug into an east-facing hillside so as to be completely underground with no visible sign of its presence over ground. It was discovered when a tractor disturbed its six flat roof slabs just below the surface.

The tomb entrance faces east-southeast. It has a short entrance passage and three internal chambers and it is not a typical passage grave.

Perhaps to compensate for the short passage and subterranean position, some archaeologists believe the builders had installed a 'lightbox' by cutting a notch in the lintel in the southeast-facing section to create a narrow gap between the uppermost roof slab. This would have allowed a ray of sunlight to shine into the tomb between early November and mid-February, closer to the autumn and spring equinoxes than to the solstices.

Because of the position of the 'lightbox', archaeologists believe the gap was created

from inside the tomb, which suggests the builders entered through the roof.

In two chambers the partial skeletal remains of four people were found. A lack of deposits on the floor of the tomb and around the entrance suggests to archaeologists that the tomb was open for a very short period, perhaps only long enough to deposit the remains and perhaps ensure that the 'lightbox' was working. The entrance inside and out was then blocked up, the 'lightbox' was blocked with clay, the roof was covered with clay and stone and the tomb was sealed for good.

CUWEEN AND WIDEFORD HILL

A different approach to manipulating light can be seen in two further passage tombs, Wideford Hill and Cuween near Kirkwall on Mainland Orkney. The two tombs face each other across the Bay of Firth.

Wideford Hill is a passage grave of the Maeshowe type, which dates from around 3000 BC. Its makers quarried into a steep hill overlooking the Bay of Firth to create a level platform on which they built the tomb. Today it appears to be made up of three concentric rings of stone but, since its earth covering was removed in the 1900s, it probably looked like a domed mound with a retaining stone wall in its day.

No human bones or pottery traces were found when it was first opened, only some animal bone. The interior had been filled to roof height with rubble and so was likely to have been deposited through the roof. The tomb was then sealed.

The passage is over five metres long and 0.60m in height and width. Off the main

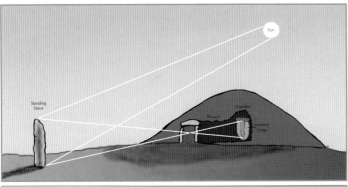

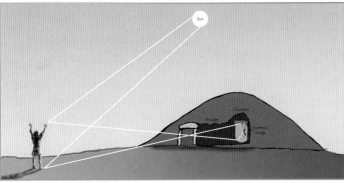

When it was excavated first in 1901, eight human skulls were found. More unusual were the remains of the skulls of 24 dogs found lying on the chamber floor, which have been found to be slightly later in date.

Even more notable is the fact that reverse alignments can be seen at Cuween and Wideford Hill tombs. When the sun is in the opposite part of the sky to the tomb entrances, the entrances fall into shadow. The shape of something standing outside the tomb entrance — a standing stone or a person — could be projected into the deepest part of the rear chamber and seen as an image on the back wall.

The process is akin to the modern camera obscura, which uses light directed through a

Above left: **Megalithic monuments often come in clusters with sightlines from monument to monument. The small aperture that allowed the sun's rays to pass through and project the image of the sun into the chamber during the 'direct alignment,' normally when the sun was on the horizon during an equinox or solstice, would also project images of distant mounds or standing stones when the sun was in the opposite quadrant of the sky — the 'reverse alignment.' Matt Gatton has proposed this served as a fertility/rebirth rite. (Matt Gatton)**

Below left: **Between the direct alignment and the reverse alignment is a window of time when the entrance to the chamber would fall into shadow while the area directly in front of the passage would still be bathed in full sunlight. At this point the mound became a 'Spirit Chamber,' projecting images of people in a seemingly ethereal form onto the backstone within the chamber. (Matt Gatton,** *The Camera Obscura and the Megalithic Tomb: The role of projected solar images in the symbolic renewal of Life.* **http://paleo-camera.com/neolithic/)**

chamber are three small side sub-chambers built into the north, east and south walls. The tomb faces west and is touched by the setting sun at the end of February.

The Cuween tomb was built into the bedrock of a hillside also. There is a main chamber with four smaller sub-chambers branching off it. The chamber is two metres high but was probably higher.

Like Wideford, Cuween dates from around 3000 BC and had been blocked up in the Neolithic. It faces onto the Bay of Firth and may have been aligned so as to be lit by the rising sun at the autumn equinox.

A long-exposure photograph showing an optical projection of a human figure upside down inside Cuween Hill passage grave.

small hole to cast an image from a lit area into a space or a dark surface. The contrast between light and dark outlines the shape or image. The human brain processes the images we see and sets them upright, as we perceive images of the world around us to be. In a darkened tomb a viewer would have seen the image upside down.

Building their tombs so as to be either directly aligned or reverse aligned with the sun would have enabled Neolithic Orcadians to cast an image from the outside — a standing stone, an adjacent tomb, a person or an animal — into the depths of a tomb. People may have waited inside to witness what they may have believed to have been an image from the other world.

This practice may give a more refined and targeted explanation for the use of swivel stones, possibly light boxes and other apertures in the structure of passage graves — perhaps not merely to control the inlet of light but to create a small hole through which images might be cast into the interior. It has been pointed out that a small hole cut into an animal skin thrown across an opening is sufficient to create darkness and project an image.

The form of inquiry that involves the observation of the behaviours of light within the chambers is called archaeo-optics, which is a sub-field of archaeo-astronomy. Archaeo-optics was co-founded by Matt Gatton and Aaron Watson.

When trying to think our way into how the Neolithic people thought about their world and the wider cosmos, the sun is prominent. In a northern, marginal environment the importance of the sun cannot be overesti-mated. The significance placed on the channelling of the sun, drawing it into the tombs, shows the effort made to control the elements in accordance with fundamental beliefs.

Tombs were aligned with key points of change in the year, the midwinter solstice being particularly significant in being a turning point to lengthening days and new growth.

It is clear that the tomb builders were using more than orientation to simply align with the sun or even to manipulate its rays at certain times of the year. The landscape and seascape were used consciously to frame or enhance the natural light.

More, the slope of the earth was co-opted. Very often there is a slope in the passage of tombs, houses and cemeteries creating what Downes has described as a 'ritual grid' to control movement or flows. This could have been aligned or linked to the principal cardinal directions or some other desired focal point. Substances or essences such as spirits, sunlight, water and people could be manipulated, going up slope and down slope in the required direction, through use of the ritual grid.

The narrow entrance ways into the stone circles at Brodgar and, at the Ness of Brodgar, the use of narrow entrances or gateways would have controlled the movement of people, animals or perhaps spirits and directed them as the builders intended. People, pathways, perhaps spirits and ancestors, could have moved downslope from the northwest or upslope from the southeast.

Architecture was used, too, in controlling and channelling elements or people. The whole of the neck of the isthmus is cut off by the Dyke of Sean, a huge monumental wall

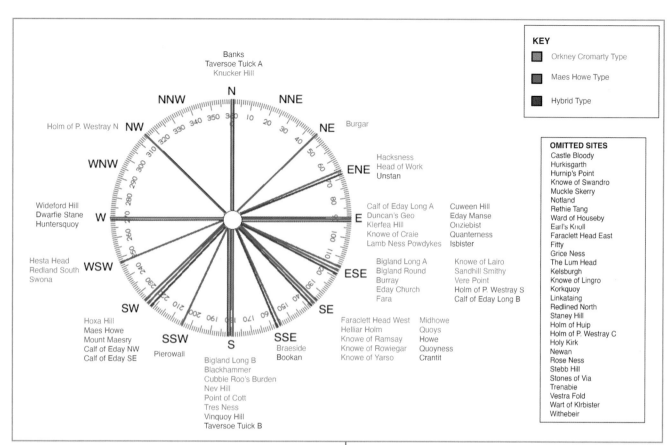

KEY

- Orkney Cromarty Type
- Maes Howe Type
- Hybrid Type

N
Banks
Taversoe Tuick A
Knucker Hill

NNW

NNE

NW Holm of P. Westray N

NE Burgar

WNW

ENE
Hacksness
Head of Work
Unstan

W
Wideford Hill
Dwarfie Stane
Huntersquoy

E
Calf of Eday Long A   Cuween Hill
Duncan's Geo   Eday Manse
Klerfea Hill   Onziebist
Knowe of Craie   Quanterness
Lamb Ness Powdykes   Isbister

WSW
Hesta Head
Redland South
Swona

ESE
Bigland Long A   Knowe of Lairo
Bigland Round   Sandhill Smithy
Burray   Vere Point
Eday Church   Holm of P. Westray S
Fara   Calf of Eday Long B

SW
Hoxa Hill
Maes Howe
Mount Maesry
Calf of Eday NW
Calf of Eday SE

SE
Faraclett Head West   Midhowe
Helliar Holm   Quoys
Knowe of Ramsay   Howe
Knowe of Rowiegar   Quoyness
Knowe of Yarso   Crantit

SSW Pierowall

S
Bigland Long B
Blackhammer
Cubbie Roo's Burden
Nev Hill
Point of Cott
Tres Ness
Vinquoy Hill
Taversoe Tuick B

SSE
Braeside
Bookan

OMITTED SITES
Castle Bloody
Hurkisgarth
Hurnip's Point
Knowe of Swandro
Muckle Skerry
Notland
Rethie Tang
Ward of Houseby
Earl's Knoll
Faraclett Head East
Fitty
Grice Ness
The Lum Head
Kelsburgh
Knowe of Lingro
Korkquoy
Linkataing
Redlined North
Staney Hill
Holm of Huip
Holm of P. Westray C
Holy Kirk
Newan
Rose Ness
Stebb Hill
Stones of Via
Trenabie
Vestra Fold
Wart of Kirbister
Withebeir

that crosses the peninsula from east to west. Geophysical survey of the Brodgar isthmus area shows evidence of disturbance, possibly structures, below ground throughout the peninsula but this stops at a defined point and certain areas around the stone circles may have been regarded as ritual spaces at which access and activity were limited.

Above: **Entrance orientation of Neolithic chambered tombs in Orkney. (Andrea Boyar)**

As well as channelling light, there may have been a concern with removing impurities from the tombs. At Maeshowe and Taversoe Tuick, a stone-lined drain had been built under the passageway that drew in sunlight — and by which the living and the dead entered. The Neolithic builders may have been withdrawing or channelling out something, whether actual or symbolic, as well as bringing something in to the tomb. It may have been associated with taking away polluting elements, or channelling spirits or water.

Maeshowe passage, drawing in sunlight, is built above a paved drain that may have channelled something out of the tomb.

52

Linking this to the realm of the living, complex settlements on Orkney had very intricate drainage systems. There may have been an analogy being drawn between people ingesting and then expelling things and houses drawing in light and then impurities having to be drawn out as well. The presence of drains in some passage tombs, as in houses, shows a concern with channelling and controlling substances and essences.

This shows a concern with the maintenance of order, the control of activity and access and, in a wider sense, with generation and regeneration through the channelling of the sun. These concerns persisted for a long time, into the Bronze Age, which showed the same emphasis on orientation of cists and barrow cemeteries, suggesting these beliefs endured.

●

Adapted by Peigín Doyle from the conference presentation by Professor Jane Downes.

Below: **The stone drain beneath the passage at Maeshowe. (Colin Richards)**

Tomnaverie stone circle with Lochnagar mountain in the background. Bronze Age people built structures to face significant points on the landscape.

(Richard Bradley)

Chapter 4:

THE PREHISTORIC SKY, 3000 BC TO 500 BC

In asking ourselves how people in prehistoric times perceived the relationship between earth, sky and their understanding of the cosmos, we must not assume that they thought only in terms of earth and sky — the upper world. We see the universe today with different eyes and our minds give us a different story to explain natural phenomena.

The relationship between earth and sky was important and Neolithic people built many structures that faced the heavens but evidence also shows a concern with the landscape around them and with the unknown place beneath the earth, from which water sprang.

Archaeologist Richard Bradley has identified many sites in Britain, especially in Scotland, that faced not the sky but significant points on the landscape. Some were not even built but were natural features that Bronze Age people adapted or 'worked' to serve their intentions.

Archaeologists often look to built structures in seeking evidence of the past but we have to shed the artificial distinction between nature and what is created by human culture and consider evidence from a wider spectrum of sources. Ancient people used and possibly deified natural features such as landforms, rocks, bodies of water, even the direction of water and, perhaps, remembered places of past rather than current significance. They built structures to face towards these features but also used the natural features themselves or modified them to create a link or point to something that they saw as important.

Early Neolithic chamber tombs tend to face the eastern part of the sky and get light at some point early in the day. Even if not getting direct sunlight, they did face east and south to the light side of the sky, rather than south and west, the dark part of the sky where the sun sets. Over time, ideas changed and this was reflected in the orientation of structures and the use of building materials. As society moved from the Late Neolithic into the Bronze Age the orientation of structures shifted from sunrise to sunset.

Although the sunrise did not lose its significance entirely, new structures had a predominantly southwesterly orientation. Monuments themselves changed, from passage tombs to stone circles and rows, burial mounds, earthworks and standing stones. In this period, hoards of metalwork, from ornaments to axes, were being deposited as offerings or to signify important places.

CLAVA CAIRNS

The Clava Cairns offer a point of departure. They are a distinct type of circular, Early Bronze Age chamber tomb found in northern Scotland, although comparable structures are known in southwest England. The Scottish cairns exhibit the change in direction from east-south to south-southwest, to face either the setting sun or the moon.

There are two sub-types of Clava Cairn in the north of Scotland; one is a corbelled passage grave with a single burial chamber and a short passage, covered with a cairn of stones. The second type is a ring cairn that

encloses an uncovered central space. A kerb often encircles the cairn and both types are surrounded by a stone circle. They are oriented towards where the mid-winter sun sets in the southwest. The standing stones are highest at the southwestern entrance and lowest in the northeast, the point directly opposite. The height grading of standing stones is an important feature of tomb orientation. Only one or two bodies have been found buried in these tombs.

A study has shown that, although cairns are found in river valleys, they were only constructed where the monuments faced a river that was running from the southwest. It is as if there was something important about that particular direction, the direction in which the sun passes across the sky in summer.

BALNARUAN OF CLAVA

At the site called Balnaruan of Clava there is a cemetery of three Clava Cairns, which stretch in a line from northeast to southwest on a ridge above the river Nairn. There may have been two other cairns originally.

The centre cairn is a ring cairn and the two end cairns are the passage grave type. The chambers were probably roofed over and the cairns much higher when they were first built. Kerbs of boulders run around the tombs and all three are surrounded by upright standing stones of different colours and heights, some of which have cupmarks.

The grave passages all face southwest. The passage of the cairn at the northeast of the group faces towards the point of sunset at the midwinter solstice. At that time, sunlight beams directly into the chamber to light up the back wall. Although the view from the southwest cairn is now blocked by a modern dwelling, the same effect would have been visible there.

Both the standing stones and the kerbstones are graded in size, with the lowest found at the northeastern part of the tombs and the highest at the southwest. Stones of different colours have been chosen for different aspects of the tombs showing a relationship between colour and sunlight. Red stones are found at the southwest, where they will reflect the ruddy light of the setting sun, while low-sized, white-coloured stones, including quartz, have been used at the northeast, which gets no

Opposite page: **The midwinter sunset viewed from the northeast passage grave at Balnaruan of Clava. (Ronnie Scott)**

Below: **The northeast passage grave at Balnaruan of Clava, one of two types of Clava cairns. (Richard Bradley)**

direct light. Such white stones might have emitted a pale glow under certain light conditions or in moonlight.

All these elements support the trend towards favouring the southwestern sky, which seems to coincide with changes in the form of monuments.

According to radiocarbon dates, the site was built around 2000 BC as a single operation whose overall design was planned in advance.

The cairns are graves first and foremost, although they are not mass, communal burials. Their design, construction and orientation show how important the site was for its builders as a place of the dead and the relationship their community believed existed between those dead and midwinter sunlight.

Above: **The southwest passage grave at Balnaruan of Clava.**

Below: **Tomnaverie stone circle under excavation.**

The site remained significant for a long time and about 1000 years after they were first built, new burials were interred in the cairns.

TOMNAVERIE

Many monuments, including tombs and stone circles, face towards points on the landscape as much as to the sun or sky. Tomnaverie is a stone circle in northeast Scotland where, again, the large boulders have been graded in height so the stones are lowest in the northeast and highest at the southwest point. This type of monument is unique to northeast Scotland.

Tomnaverie sits on a low hill. Built in the very Early Bronze Age, the site was developed in a series of phases, starting with fires whose burnt remains formed a low mound. Sometime between 2600 BC and 2000 BC, the mound was built over with a ring cairn, open at the centre and over 15m across, which was surrounded by a kerb. A bank of rubble was built up around the monument to create a platform.

Later again, a stone circle, which is about 17m across, was erected around the cairn within the rubble platform. It originally consisted of 12 stones, of which two stones have been lost, and a recumbent, or lying, stone at the southwest, which blocks the entrance and is flanked by two tall upright stones.

The stone circle encloses the inner cairn with its boulder kerb. The kerbstones in the earlier cairn were graded in height to favour the southwest before the stone circle was built likewise, so this emphasis on the southwest must have been a dominant idea over a long period. The grading in height enhances the impact of the monument.

The recumbent stone is whinstone with some quartz seams, while four of the circle stones are light-red granite. The kerb, too, shows the use of different coloured stones, some of which have cupmarks. Attention was given also to the northeast side possibly suggesting an opposing or complementary significance. Here the smaller stones are set closer together and beneath the outer platform at the foot of the kerb six sherds of Beaker pottery were placed. The insertion of a recumbent or lying stone at the southwest may have been to frame a particular view or focal point for the monument or a solar or lunar event.

The design and orientation of the cairn and circle reflect the beliefs and rituals of its builders in the Bronze Age but the importance given to the site persisted over a very long time. Around 1000 BC, cremated human bones were placed in the centre of the cairn. Much later, in the 16th or 17th century AD, a pit was dug in the centre of the cairn and fires were lit on its summit, showing the site still had significance for people in the area. It may have been used as a beacon, a common practice at the time.

Although the orientation clearly favours the southwest and midwinter sunset, the real focal point for Tomnaverie is the dramatic Lochnagar mountain to the southwest. Viewed from within the monument, the recumbent stone frames the mountain.

Lochnagar is a peak in the Grampian mountains, which stretch from northeast to southwest in the Scottish Highlands. The name Lochnagar refers to a small loch or corrie found on its northeast side around which the peaks are grouped. Another of its names in Scots Gàidhlig was *Beinn Chìochan* or 'mountain of the breasts'.

The re-erected recumbent stone and flankers at Tomnaverie frame Lochnagar mountain.

(Richard Bradley)

six standing stones. In the Late Bronze Age, a massive earthwork was added with a deep inner ditch nearly three metres wide and an outer bank five metres wide, which was revetted on the inside by a low kerb.

The monument is unusual in that it has some of the characteristics of a small henge along with the features of a late stone circle.

Although the circle faces southwest, it is aligned across the valley on the flank of the Midmill Neolithic long cairn.

Looking towards Tomnaverie from the southwest, it is easily visible on the skyline sitting on its stone ridge. This may have been a particular consideration at the time when fires were being lit.

HILL OF TUACH

On the southwestern slope of the Hill of Tuach in Aberdeenshire is a small henge comprising a stone circle with a ring ditch. It overlooks Tuach burn, a small tributary of the river Don.

Built in two phases, the Early Bronze Age stage saw two zones of cremation in a cremation cemetery around which a stone circle was built. In its original form the ring comprised

---

Above: **Excavated pits, some with cremation burials, inside the enclosure at Tuach. (Aaron Watson)**

Right: **Croft Moraig stone circle, with Schiehallion mountain in the background. (Aaron Watson)**

CROFT MORAIG

Unlike the Hill of Tuach, Croft Moraig stone circle, at the head of Loch Tay, near Aberfeldy, Scotland, held few, if any, human remains (the burnt bone was too small to be identified). It does face southwest but not to the sun.

Croft Moraig in some ways seems a typical stone circle. It was a man-made structure but recent excavations have shown the central point to be a large, glacial erratic boulder, found not built, which was adapted to form the core of the built monument.

The monument consists of five elements; a rounded mound incorporating a natural glacial boulder; a stone circle of nine boulders, four of which have fallen, two portal stones standing outside the main circle, an inner oval of eight standing stones and an outer ring of boulders that may have been a bank.

Beneath the surface there was a ring of timber posts linked to a shallow ditch around part of the perimeter and two postholes that could have been the remains of an entrance or porch.

Following an excavation in 1965, it was thought the site had been built in three phases over a possible period of 1000 years, based on pottery finds of a small amount of Carinated Bowl dating from the Neolithic and the existence of the timber circle, which was likely to predate the stone structures.

However, nearly all the pottery from Croft Moraig is of a type that dates to the Middle to Late Bronze Age and the Neolithic sherds were found with the Bronze Age pottery. Recent excavation at sites in Scotland and Northern Ireland have uncovered a type of Middle Bronze Age house called a ring ditch house, which dates from the same time as the pottery and whose shape and size follow closely the outline of post holes under the stones.

Based on more recent excavation findings, a revised view saw the site as developing in the Early Bronze Age with the outer stone circle followed in the Bronze Age by the internal ring of postholes, the timber porch and the shallow ditch, which are seen as the remains of a ring ditch house. The final phase was the insertion of upright stones into the refilled ditch that followed the outline of the outer bank of rubble.

In this time sequence the first stone circle and the ring ditch house faced east-southeast. When the oval of boulders and the outer boundary were built, the orientation was changed to south-southwest and marked by the incorporation of a decorated stone on the perimeter.

The glacial boulder at the centre of the monument is smooth, polished schist scored by glacial ice. Naturally coloured bands ranging from blue-green and creamy-yellow to orange cross its surface and mark it as different from the stone material found in the local landscape. The colour contrast between the central stone and the stones used in the ring would have been noticeable and the choice of contrasting stones for the outer circle may have been deliberate. The outer stone circle was built around the distinctive glacial stone.

The low mound on which the stone structures had been set was identified as a natural glacial mound. This had been shaped deliberately on the east and west to increase its height to form a ramp rising towards the southwest at the time the outer wall was built.

The midsummer sunset behind Schiehallion viewed
from Croft Moraig. (Richard Bradley)

Cupmarks can be seen on several stones in the monument including a long stone on the southern edge of the monument. The fact that it is lying on soil rather than on the rubble foundation and faces towards south-southwest suggests that it might have been inserted later across the entrance of the oval stone structure to mark the end of its use.

The question arises, why was the natural setting chosen in the first place and then shaped to rise in a southwesterly direction?

The answer rears up 11kms away — the peak of Schiehallion mountain in the Southern Highlands range. Viewed from the erratic at the heart of the monument the sun can be seen setting near the peak of Schiehallion at the midsummer solstice. Marking the other point of the year, midwinter solstice, the long axis of the inner oval of stones faces to the setting sun in the southwest.

In Scottish folklore Schiehallion, in Gàidhlig *Sidh Chaillean* or the Summit of the Caledonians, is the centre of Scotland. The mountain is hard quartzite stone formed by the pressures of ice in the Ice Ages. On its southern side is a network of caves in a band of softer limestone that runs along Gleann Mor. The caves are the subject of folklore about supernatural beings and one, *Uamh Tom a' Mhor-fir* (Cave of the Great Man) was believed to be the entrance to the underworld.

Schiehallion also was said to be the place of the mythical *Cailleach Bheur,* The Blue Witch, who appeared at Hallowe'en to bring in the winter.

It is possible that people noticed this sunset effect on Schiehallion from the glacial mound and erratic at a very early time and then, some time later, the ring of boulders was built around the mound and the coloured stone at its centre, to highlight the event and create a link. The effect was heightened by grading the boulders of the stone oval and circle, and shaping the natural glacial mound, so they pointed south-southwest. Scatterings of quartz inside the structure would have added to the effect.

Croft Moraig was found and adapted rather than man-made. The people at the time adapted something remarkable that they found in the landscape to create and emphasize a connection, not just with sunlight but with an important point on the horizon, which must have been part of their beliefs on the landscape and an otherworld that was there though perhaps not seen.

BEN LAWERS

Near Croft Moraig is another significant mountain, Ben Lawers. It lies to the north of Loch Tay from which flows the longest river in Scotland. As the highest mountain in the Southern Highlands, it is a geological formation, but ancient people made it a repository of stone art or rock carvings, making a 'natural' monument of something already in the landscape.

Over 100 decorated rocks have been recorded there. Many are on high ground and in areas in which there are no other prehistoric monuments.

The rock art sites are mostly on the north shore of the loch looking southward. They do not overlook the entire loch but mainly that section that stretches from northeast to southwest, which is the path of the sun as it crosses the sky. The main group of carved

rocks face in two directions, those of the rising sun at the northeast and of the setting sun in the southwest.

The top of one decorated outcrop had a large natural basin at its upper side. Complex designs had been carved into two sides of the basin and worked and broken quartz was found at its base. The pecked art faces northeast along the loch and glitters brightly in the rising sun.

Another large, domed rock with a platform in front of it faces in the opposite direction. A set of concentric circles were incised on its highest point. There are two types of rock and the one that sparkles in light has received the greatest attention. The several hammerstones found here suggest that people might have been working or 'pounding' the rock to make it glitter even more.

Another element, water, should not be overlooked. The hills and rocks look down over a body of water that reflects the sky and

the light of the passing sun at a point where the loch follows what seems to be a propitious direction.

The location and decoration of selected rocks suggest a relationship between light, rock, art and direction or orientation of natural features.

An exploratory project on Ben Lawers saw archaeologists dig test pits against the sides of decorated rocks and another set of trial pits five metres away. This was to discover if decorated rocks were linked to any artefacts and, if so, what light they might throw on why the rocks had been carved and how they might have been used.

Opposite page: **Decorated outcrop on Ben Lawers, looking northeast with Loch Tay in the background. (Aaron Watson)**

Above: **Decorated outcrop on Ben Lawers overlooking Loch Tay. (Aaron Watson)**

Below: **Outcrop with recently discovered motifs on Ben Lawers, with Loch Tay in the background. (Aaron Watson)**

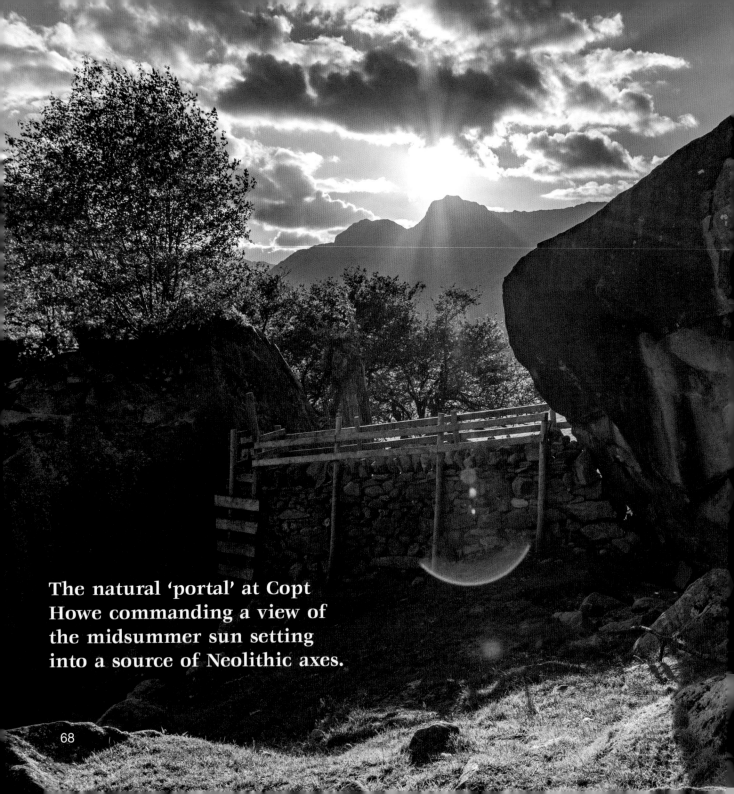

The natural 'portal' at Copt Howe commanding a view of the midsummer sun setting into a source of Neolithic axes.

The results found that artefacts were associated with decorated outcrops rather than the other rocks. This held true regardless of what patterns were incised on the rocks.

Other elements of interconnected relations can be seen here, for example, a relationship between the complexity of rock art and its location in the landscape. The more complex carvings, with many concentric rings, tend to be on higher ground and visible over a wide area. Simpler patterns, with single and double rings and cups, are usually found on lower ground in areas suitable for habitation, although this pattern is not found everywhere in Great Britain.

Decorated rocks may have acted also as markers within a landscape to indicate paths or strategic or significant places.

COPT HOWE

At Copt Howe, in the Langdale valley in Cumbria, northwest England, the gap between two huge natural boulders faces directly towards Harrison Stickle and Loft Crag, major sources of Neolithic polished stone axes in ancient Britain.

Langdale axes were greatly prized and were traded widely. Axe production at Langdale started at the beginning of the Neolithic period and ended around 3400 BC.

The passage is also naturally aligned towards the setting sun at midsummer as it passes across Harrison Stickle and sets in its side. In 3000 BC, the sun would have passed behind and over the mountain, lighting it.

Although not a built passage, the gap between the two massive stones creates a natural alignment to a place of significance to ancient people.

The Copt Howe boulders have natural markings similar to cupmarks but the people who found this site did decorate the sides of the boulders that formed the passage. The motifs are spirals and concentric circles similar to Irish megalithic art motifs rather than to British rock art.

At the foot of the main panel of carved art, a drystone platform one metre wide was built at some time in the Neolithic, with a foundation of large boulders and a capping of flat stones. Placed against the foot of the rock were stone tools, punches, likely to have been used in making the motifs. The tools were made from the same glacial rock in the area, which means the designs were made with rocks found at the spot. Sealed beneath that layer, at Neolithic ground surface level, were found more art motifs of concentric circles and spirals.

Below: **The main decorated panel at Copt Howe after excavation. (Aaron Watson)**

As motifs associated with the dead at Irish sites like Newgrange, the art must have had powerful meaning. The passage may have acted as both an entrance, and a barrier, to an important landscape.

HOARDS

As the new technology of metalworking spread, Bronze Age people found another way of marking a significant place in the landscape while also observing the solar calendar. Collections of valuable objects started to be placed at important or ritual places. Often, they were swords, daggers, axes, shields, jewellery, pins and tools in bronze or gold but there is evidence that organic items like leather, wood, jet, amber and textiles were deposited at times.

In the Early Bronze Age, there was a trade in copper axes from southwest Ireland into Scotland. Goods were moved across the Irish Sea into western Britain and along the Great Glen into northeast Scotland.

We do not know exactly what made a site significant, though hoards were often left in water, in rivers, lakes and bogs. Some sites seem to have had strategic geographic importance. A hoard containing three separate deposits of metal axe heads, knives and daggers was left at *Dail na Caraidh* (the field of the fish trap) near Fort William, Scotland. The findspot sits at the southern end of the Great Glen where the head of Scotland's longest sea loch, Loch Linne, would have ended during the Bronze Age.

Within view of the site was the highest mountain in Britain, Ben Nevis. The sun rises out of the mountain range at the winter solstice, the shortest day in the year.

CULTURE AND LANDSCAPE

The morning sunrise had been important since the beginning of the Neolithic period but, by the Bronze Age, there was a greater emphasis on the sunset. It was expressed in many structures other than passage graves. Nor was orientation concerned only with the dead and with the sun.

Natural features in the landscape became important, water held significance and even certain directions seemed to have had favourable or unfavourable connotations.

Certain features or phenomena in the landscape must have seemed strange to the ancient people. They may have decided to emphasize the importance of a place that seemed outside normal explanation by building a monument to face in its direction or place valuable objects there to show reverence.

Below: **Digital reconstruction of the midwinter sun rising behind the Nevis range as seen from the position of the Dail na Caraidh metalwork hoard. (Aaron Watson)**

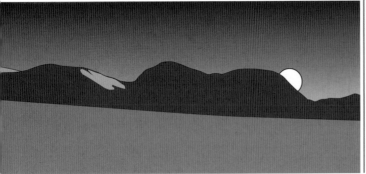

In some cases, though not all, there was a link with the dead and with some aspect of the sun's movements. Rock art panels at sites that are aligned on solar phenomena do not necessarily have a funerary context.

We have to ask not what was the relationship between the dead and the sky in the world view of ancient people but what did they think the cosmos to be.

Most world religions share the notion that there are three worlds, the present world, the other or lower world of the dead and the upper world of the deities or existence after death. From their surviving structures and artefacts Bronze Age people showed concern with aspects of the natural landscape and the world underground as much as with the sky.

Places of transition between the different tiers of worlds, or where one world seemed to impinge on the other, were places of significance, often marked by cemeteries, deposits or monuments.

Water and rivers seemed to have held a special importance. Water is both under this world as it emerges in springs and it reflects the upper world on its surface. It may have been perplexing or to have had supernatural qualities; it flowed in rivers and lakes yet appeared from underground at times and other times fell from the sky. How to explain its permeable surface, its ability to mirror the sky and the landscape, to give life but to take it at times?

Certain sites were emphasized because springs or rivers were associated with them or they were altered to mimic naturally occurring water. Springs occur in large henges in southern England; the henge and stone circles at Avebury are beside Silbury Hill, the source of an important tributary of the Thames; in the landscape of the Boyne valley there are ritual ponds.

Even certain directions are perceived as propitious, some not. In the Arctic, the north is associated with the dead. Few tombs in Ireland and Britain face in that direction. The sun travels across the sky between northeast to southwest at different times of year. Lakes or rivers that follow this direction have been marked by the decoration of stones on the mountains overlooking them.

There seemed to have been a relationship, at times, between the landscape, the skyline, the sun and the materials used in building, with red stones to the southwest to reflect the setting sun or a stone circle built around a distinctive, coloured boulder.

To assume that marking natural features or orienting structures was solely concerned with the sun or planets as calendars to announce the turning points of the year is to forget that you cannot build a monument to predict a movement of stars or planets in the sky until you know already that it is there. Then you do not need a monument to act as an observatory.

Given such surviving evidence of Bronze Age culture and practices, archaeologists in the quest for explanations have to change their views and examine the meaning of natural features that ancient people found and adapted to their needs rather than the traditional focus on built structures.

●

Adapted by Peigín Doyle from the conference presentation by Professor Richard Bradley.

One of the two chambers of Dowth passage tomb at Brú na Bóinne.

Chapter 5:

SKYSCAPE, CULTURE AND THE IRISH PASSAGE TOMB TRADITION: A COMPLEX LEGACY

During the last Ice Age, about 20,000 years before present, a sheet of ice up to 900m thick covered the whole of Ireland. Only the isolated tips of mountain peaks, with a total area of about 100 sq. km, pushed themselves above the glacial landscape. These pinpoints of land were located mostly in the areas around the Comeragh Mountains in County Waterford and the Galtee Mountains in County Tipperary. Given these conditions, Ireland was colonized by flora and fauna and settled by humans much later than its neighbour Britain, which remained largely unglaciated over its southern region during that era.

The ending of the Ice Age left an island with an elevationally lower interior of sodden and swampy ground. Much, much later, when humans had settled and begun to build, where they chose to erect their burial tombs generally avoided the inhospitable central lowland. A picture of Ireland plotted according to the location of court, passage, portal and wedge tombs would show an empty interior with megalithic monuments hugging the high ground. Only when ringforts came to be built in the Early Medieval, AD 400 onwards, does this 'empty quarter' start to intensively fill with evidence of human structures.

Across the island, there are almost 1400 tombs comprising five different types, court,

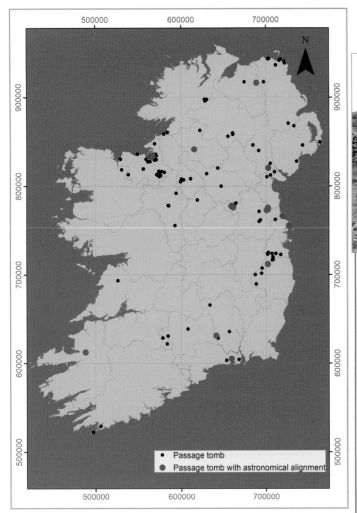

might say about the thinking of their builders. This project involved visiting about 300 sites including related hilltop cairns and megalithic structures, many in remote locations. Astronomical surveys of tombs that had passages in good condition were also measured. Interestingly, many of these tombs, or their mountainous landscapes, have been surrounded by myth and folklore from the Neolithic onward.

Ireland's most developed passage tombs are elaborate feats of engineering achievement, decorated with superb megalithic art. Their circular mounds are surrounded by a kerb of adjoining boulders with a passage leading into an internal funerary chamber crowned by a corbelled roof in many cases. Less complex forms of tomb design occur but

Above: **Doonaveeragh passage tomb, Co Sligo, a summit burial site. (Frank Prendergast)**

Above left: **Distribution of Irish passage tombs. (Frank Prendergast)**

portal, passage, wedge and Linkardstown. Passage tombs in particular are thought to reflect a more complex cosmology than is expressed in the other categories.

Dr Frank Prendergast has surveyed all the passage tombs in Ireland for their distribution patterns, intervisibility, orientation to sky phenomena and landscapes, and what this

Winter solstice sunrise from the east tomb of Knockroe passage grave.

The main passage tomb at
Knowth, Brú na Bóinne, with
some of its satellite tombs.

all have a passage into an interior space.

Passage tombs are encountered predominantly on locally high ground and on the summits of mountains, generally grouped in dense or dispersed clusters. The majority were built mainly between 3300 BC–2900 BC with some as early as 3750 BC. They have been found in the north, east and south of the country and 230 are recorded to date. Many have been destroyed in the intervening millennia by human action.

In Ireland, the chambers of passage tombs vary in shape; there are undifferentiated (no obvious chamber), round, polygonal or the more elaborate cruciform shapes. Cruciform means a main central chamber flanked by a left and right smaller chamber known as a cell or recess. A symmetrically placed end-cell completes the design style. Also in Ireland, the right-hand cell is nearly always larger than that on the left. Cruciform tombs are much more common in Ireland than in other parts of Europe.

Many passage tombs are decorated with abstract art carved or picked onto the structural stones. Motifs are described as geometrical or abstract and still defy attempts to decode their meaning. However, recent archaeological research shows that certain motif styles were deliberately placed at key architectural junctions within a tomb. Many cells are found to hold massive stone basins, some decorated, containing the deposited remains of the dead, along with artefacts like bone pins, pottery, stone beads, pendants and small stone balls. Structural stones along the passages, chambers, sills and even unseen in the roofing stones can carry elaborate carved or incised ornamentation.

The direction of the burial chamber, passage and entrance can have huge architectural and symbolic importance. The entrance and passage would have been intended not just for access but probably for religious ritual or formal ceremony. Such practices may have involved processional movement, linked to ideas about power, life, death and the place of the living and the dead within the cosmos.

PASSAGE TOMB CLUSTERS

Topography, horizon, focus and orientation were critical elements in the placement and alignment of Irish passage tombs. While every structure inevitably has orientation, the term alignment signifies intentionality on the part of the builder to face a target of some kind.

A preference for clustering and siting on high ground or mountain summits are addi-

Above: **One of 30 surviving monuments at Carrowmore, Co Sligo. (Frank Prendergast)**

77

elevated east-west ridges that cut across the Cúil Irra peninsula.

The Carrowkeel complex in the Bricklieve Mountains, County Sligo, has 16 passage tombs spread across a number of hills, of which Drumnagranshy tomb on the summit of Kesh Corann (359m) is the highest.

The landscape of Slieve na Calliagh, Loughcrew, County Meath, has 17 passage tombs, 15 cairns and other unclassified mega-lithic structures aggregated on three hilltop summits — Carnbane East, Carnbane West and Patrickstown. Slieve na Calliagh is the highest summit in Meath and affords commanding views of the countryside in all directions.

In County Donegal, the adjacent townlands of Kilmonaster Middle and Croaghan have a notable cluster, with ten passage tombs originally located close to the summit of Kilmonaster Hill. Several others are dispersed to the east with one crowning the summit of the nearby Croaghan Hill.

HEIGHT AND AUTHORITY

The pattern of siting and alignment of passage tombs and their entrances shows a concern with height, height difference and a desire to face their entrances towards targets of likely symbolic importance. On a national scale, of the 136 tombs with an extant passage surveyed to date by Prendergast, nearly 70 were found to be aligned at other cairns or passage tombs in the landscape, with each target being elevationally higher in every case.

At Loughcrew, for example, six of the 12 tombs whose passages can be discerned on Carnbane West face towards the focal hill of Carnbane East with Cairn T on its summit.

tional defining features. Across Ireland, there are five main sites with passage tomb clusters: Brú na Bóinne, County Meath, includes three clusters of passage tombs at Newgrange, Knowth and Dowth with at least 40 known tombs and many related structures. Brú na Bóinne and its monuments sit on a shale ridge overlooking a pronounced bend in the Boyne river.

Carrowmore, County Sligo, with over 30 remaining monuments, originally 64, is not on a mountain summit but does sit on two

Above: **Carrowkeel E passage tomb, Co Sligo, facing Queen Maeve's cairn on Knocknarea. (Frank Prendergast)**

Opposite page: **Slieve Donard, Co Down, where the once-highest passage tomb in northwest Europe was located. (Frank Prendergast)**

This 35m-diameter cairn is at the centre of the Loughcrew complex. At Carrowmore, five tombs face inward towards the central ridge and encircle the central tomb, Listoghil (Carrowmore 51). At Carrowkeel, tombs E, G, K and H are aligned towards Queen Maeve's Cairn on top of Knocknarea mountain in the Cúil Irra peninsula. At Knowth, the main passage tomb is ringed by 20 smaller satellite tombs, 'looking' inward towards the central tomb in nearly every case.

Nationally, there is a general pattern that where one tomb looks towards another similar monument or a mountain peak the target tomb or cairn is higher than the 'viewing' tomb as previously described.

Preference for height may reflect a wish for such tombs to dominate the terrain and to be visible from afar. As well as the funerary role of the monument, their builders seem to have been concerned with the paired concept of higher and lower, possibly indicating hierarchy and power. There also may have been a perception that the higher tomb had more authority in the landscape than ones lower down, perhaps being the burial place of the socially elite.

Did the builders use monumentality as a statement of their presence or to engage in some way with the sky, as part of a wider cosmology? Slieve Donard, County Down, which was destroyed in 1826 during the principal triangulation for the Trigonometrical Survey of Ireland, was originally about 25m in diam-

Thomastown passage tomb, Co Meath, is aligned to Cairn T, Loughcrew, at summer solstice sunset.

(Ken Williams)

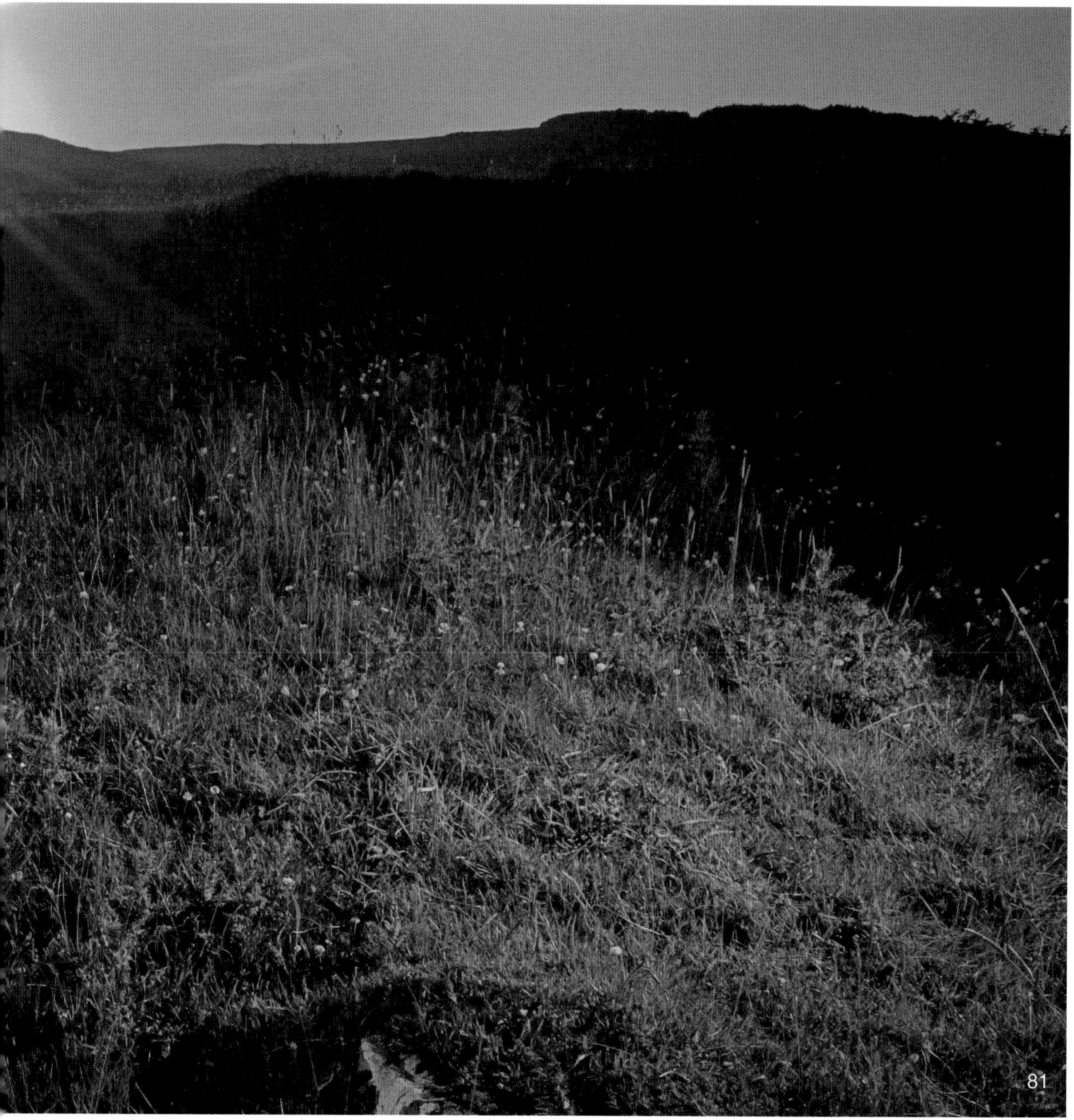

eter, the highest passage tomb not only in Ireland but in northwest Europe. Its height (853m) and visibility in the landscape must have made it a very eminent monument for the people who made it.

SOLAR ALIGNMENT

Solar alignment is another recurring feature of passage tomb alignment in Ireland and elsewhere. Such occurrences raise key archaeological questions in relation to reasoning and world-view in the Neolithic. Curiously, Irish passage tombs face to all points around the compass. Statistical analysis shows no predominant pattern or preference in the orientation of their chambers and passages if looked at in this manner. This demonstrates how there is no substitute for human observation in the field.

Of the 136 tombs with a surviving chamber or passage surveyed and analyzed by Prendergast, 22 indicated a possibly deliberate alignment on the sun at astronomically important times of the year. Seventeen are aligned on sunrise or sunset at the solstices, with seven of these facing summer solstice and 10 to the winter solstice. These include Slieve Gullion, south cairn, County Armagh, which is aligned on the setting sun at the winter solstice. From within the chamber the sun is seen to simultaneously set behind Loughcrew passage tomb cemetery more than 60 kilometres distant.

Thomastown passage tomb, County Meath, three kilometres southeast of Loughcrew, is also aligned to Loughcrew Hill. The remnants of its passage face Cairn T, the highest tomb in the complex, and, most dramatically,

summer solstice sunset behind Carnbane East and Cairn T in the northwest.

At Newgrange in the Boyne valley complex, the passage is aligned to the rising sun at winter solstice, an event that is one of the most remarkable and beautiful examples of the phenomenon of sunlight animating the chamber of a passage tomb.

The southern tomb at Dowth in the Boyne valley is also illuminated at winter solstice sunset while the nearby tomb at Townleyhall, County Louth, faces sunrise at summer solstice.

At Carrowkeel, Tomb G is aligned close, though not directly, to summer solstice sunset. Cairn G (and possibly Cairn F) is the only known Irish passage tomb, other than Newgrange, to possess a slot above the

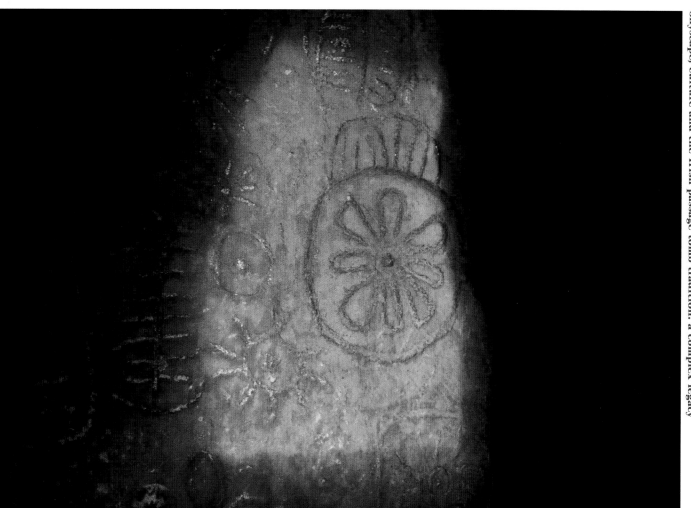

entrance lintel stone. Nearby, Tomb H is now known to have an alignment on summer solstice sunset.

Nationally, five passage tombs have an orientation on either sunrise or sunset coinciding with the times of equinox. Cairn T, Loughcrew, aligned on sunrise at the spring

Above: **The backstone of Cairn T passage tomb, Co Meath, is illuminated at vernal and autumnal equinox. (Ken Williams)**

Opposite page: **Carrowkeel G passage tomb, Co Sligo, with roof slot above the lintel stone. (Frank Prendergast)**

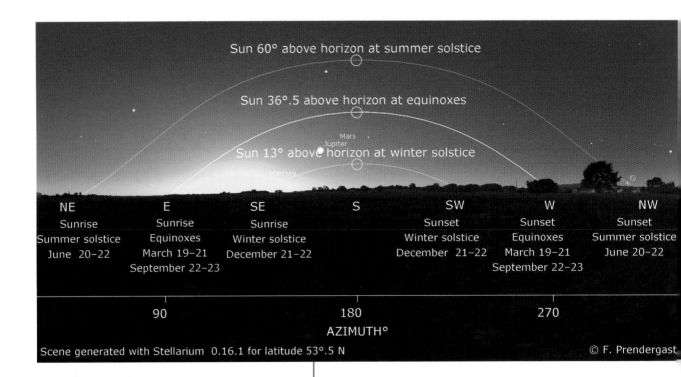

Sun 60° above horizon at summer solstice

Sun 36°.5 above horizon at equinoxes

Mars
Jupiter
Sun 13° above horizon at winter solstice

Mercury

NE	E	SE	S	SW	W	NW
Sunrise	Sunrise	Sunrise		Sunset	Sunset	Sunset
Summer solstice	Equinoxes	Winter solstice		Winter solstice	Equinoxes	Summer solstice
June 20–22	March 19–21	December 21–22		December 21–22	March 19–21	June 20–22
	September 22–23				September 22–23	

90   180   270

AZIMUTH°

Scene generated with Stellarium 0.16.1 for latitude 53°.5 N   © F. Prendergast

and autumn equinoxes, is a spectacular example of this phenomenon.

A number of passage tombs have a southerly orientation and, conversely, a noticeable number are orientated in the opposite direction, broadly north. At Carrowkeel, for example, the largest cairn, Cairn F, is aligned north towards the nearby Cairn E.

In some cultures, and it may have been the case with our own ancestors, the northern region was associated with death. The view to the northern horizon may have been linked to a belief that the spirits of the dead passed into the sky in that direction, a zone lying distinctly beyond the northerly rising and setting limits of the sun on summer solstice.

Moving into the Bronze Age, significant points in the moon's cycle are marked at some monuments, including stone row alignments. These occurrences probably were linked to ritual practices.

There are patterns other than astronomical to consider in terms of prehistoric monument alignment. Many features in the landscape may have had sacred significance for ancient cultures and served as culturally meaningful targets. These can be natural features, other structures or even directions known only to the builders. Many tombs are orientated towards or parallel to a ridge or a river. Sacred spaces, valleys, hills and rivers all seem to have been important factors in the selection of location or alignment.

ASTRONOMICAL SIGNIFICANCE

The disparate set of directions found in the orientation of Irish passage tombs raises the question of whether these are random or deliberate and what, if any, was their astronomical significance.

The direction of sunrise and sunset at solstice can be easily marked by observation, sky watching, with reference to any noticeable and remembered point in the landscape or on the horizon. Afterwards, sunrise or sunset directions can be tracked as a recurring event in later years. This would have allowed for such happenings to be anticipated and any ceremonies and rituals planned for, assuming the sun was ever used in such a fashion.

Equinox, which falls midway between winter and summer solstice, would have been less easy to establish. There is no observable event in the sky to mark it, unlike the standstill of the sun at winter solstice. Nevertheless, around the equinoxes, sunrise and sunset directions are almost directly opposed, being due east and due west, with day and night being, experientially at least, of equal duration. Although instances of tomb alignment to the sun at equinox does happen, statistically, such examples are weakly encountered in the archaeological record. Consequently, equinox

Below: **Astronomy of solstice — the sun approaches standstill at winter solstice. (Frank Prendergast)**

Opposite page: **The sun's path across the sky throughout the year. (Frank Prendergast)**

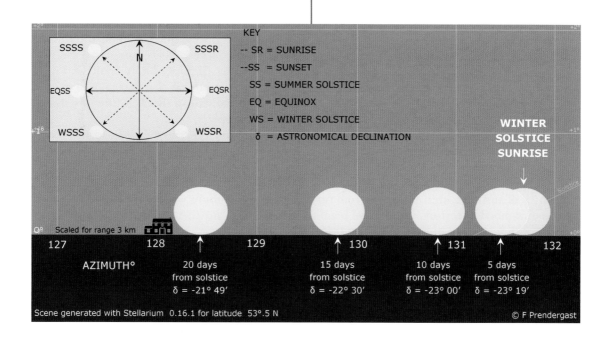

KEY
-- SR = SUNRISE
--SS = SUNSET
SS = SUMMER SOLSTICE
EQ = EQUINOX
WS = WINTER SOLSTICE
δ = ASTRONOMICAL DECLINATION

SSSS SSSR
EQSS EQSR
WSSS WSSR

WINTER SOLSTICE SUNRISE

Scaled for range 3 km

127   128   129   130   131   132

AZIMUTH°

20 days from solstice δ = -21° 49'

15 days from solstice δ = -22° 30'

10 days from solstice δ = -23° 00'

5 days from solstice δ = -23° 19'

Scene generated with Stellarium 0.16.1 for latitude 53°.5 N

© F Prendergast

may have held less powerful cultural or religious symbolism for the tomb builders.

However, where a tomb is so aligned the result can provide a spectacular display of solar illumination within the burial chamber, especially of any megalithic art. Cairn T, Loughcrew, is a magnificent example of equinoctial orientation towards sunrise at the equinoxes, channelling the sun's light into the tomb chamber in late March and September. The motifs on the richly decorated backstone in the end recess appear breathtakingly beautiful at such times. Such events still inspire us and draw onlookers, millennia after they were first conceived. However, although inspiring wonder, such examples are comparatively rare.

Any fixation on the idea of alignment towards rising or setting heavenly bodies pushes discussion in the direction of what the builders were looking for out in the heavens. Given that the pre-eminent concern of the tomb was for containment of the cremated remains of the dead within, additional concerns might have been with what the remains of the dead, the spirits, were receiving from the sun and the role of sunlight illuminating the tomb for a defined period of time.

Direct light from the sun at sunrise and sunset, especially entering a passage tomb aligned to solstice or equinox, would have been charged with powerful symbolism. Perhaps the entry of sunlight, shining on the remains of the entombed ancestors, would have been a means of dialogue between the dead and the deified sun. Its warmth and light might have imparted something to the dead within the chamber, maybe the promise of renewed life. So, birth, life, death and renewal may have been perceived as replicating the annual cycle

similar to the seasonal dying away of vegetation followed, after an interval, by new growth.

Perhaps it was seen as warming the souls of the dead or strengthening the deceased for the journey to the afterlife. To ensure these processes, you needed alignment on the sun. However, was alignment a mechanism for achieving something else that people may have believed within their culture or religious belief system?

At the solstices, the direction of the rising and setting sun appears to slow and stand still on the horizon for about a week. This is because of the tilt of the earth's axis. If the passage of a tomb were to be aligned on the direction of sunrise or sunset at such times,

Above: **The Paps of Anu, Co Kerry, crowned by two possible passage tombs. Most tombs surveyed had sight of the distant northern horizon. (Frank Prendergast)**

it would enjoy the presence of direct solar illumination in the passage and chamber on a greater number of days than at any other time in the year.

Because of the earth's elliptical orbit, we are also closer by about five million kilometres to the sun around the time of the winter solstice than at the summer solstice. This makes the sun's disc appear larger in mid-winter by about three per cent and sunrise and sunset can seem brighter and more spectacular as a result.

Using alignment on sunrise or sunset at the solstices so as to prolong the presence of sunlight inside the tomb might have amplified perceived symbolic meaning and, thereby, increased the religious and ritual significance of such aligned tombs on the landscape, and for the people of the time.

Cultural astronomy is concerned with these questions. It examines the social matrix that archaeological data supplies so as to find meaning in the role and function of our ancestors' structures free from biases resulting from our modern world-view.

What did our ancestors perceive when they looked out on their world?

It is thought they might have believed in a three-tiered cosmos consisting of landscape, underworld and skyscape. In the Neolithic the horizon might have been imagined as the unreachable boundary between landscape, skyscape and the underworld, dividing the natural world from the supernatural world. This may have imbued such vistas with mystery, meaning and power. For these reasons, certain sectors of the present-day horizon need protection from intrusive development; such vistas are part of our cultural heritage.

The horizon is the zone where the sun, planets and stars seem to begin and end their apparent journeys. Out of the underworld, and framed by the horizon, celestial bodies appear to rise, travel in a predictable path across the sky and then set in the opposite horizon into the underworld again. On every horizon, it is also comparatively easy to mark the most northerly and southerly limits of the sun's journey. These solstitial points or markers, spaced six months apart, must have held enormous significance in a ritual sense.

Of the 300 sites surveyed by Prendergast, further spatial analysis of horizon distances surrounding the tombs and related cairns strongly indicates that the majority have visibility of the most distant horizon in the northerly direction, in other words, tombs were located so as to ensure the farthest possible view of the horizon beyond the northerly rising and setting limits of the sun.

Passage tombs must have had a critical role in the cosmology of our ancestors in several respects, not just for containment of the remains of the dead and their grave goods but as a focus for ceremonial rituals, facilitating the passage of the spirit to the afterlife and links to the passage of the seasons.

The builders would have been easily able to anticipate the predictable apparent movement of the sun along the horizon as well as its return to specific limiting directions at certain key points in the year.

They did not need to use tombs as instruments or observatories to measure or track time, as is sometimes claimed. As human society moved into the Bronze Age, 2400 BC–800 BC, there is archaeological and statistical evidence of more advanced ritual practices in

Entrance to Newgrange passage tomb. The primary concern of passage tombs was containment of the remains of the dead.

(Ken Williams)

the alignment patterns of other monument types. These are linked to the much more complicated and changing periodic phases and movements of the moon, monthly and annually over an 18.6-year cycle.

Any preoccupation of the passage tomb builders with facing their burial structures towards the sun, at critical times of the year in some cases, probably is explained best as being a part of a wider understanding and engagement with the cosmos. It may even have been that the sun itself was not deified or worshipped in itself but was a symbol of some other process that was part of their world view. Other considerations, such as marking seasons as part of the agricultural cycle, were probably determined with recourse to annually recurring changes in environmental factors and nature, all very familiar to farming communities.

So, when seeking broader meaning in passage tomb architecture, landscape siting and ritual use, astronomical interpretations are but one of many plausible alternative factors. Relatedly, any attempt by modern investigators to probe the Neolithic mind might be best guided by Gabriel Cooney's idea of 'complex'. He advocates this term to better capture the broader meaning of prehistoric tombs and the 'range of ceremonial purposes that these groups of monuments played'. The literal meaning of the term is used here merely to highlight the many challenges facing investigators when interpreting megalithic architecture.

There can be little doubt that people in the prehistoric past engaged with the starry elements of their skyscape. But any attempt at definitive interpretations of such distant cul-

tural history must be hypothetical, guided by good investigative science and, tantalizingly, inevitably remain shrouded in much mystery.

●

Adapted by Peigín Doyle from the conference presentation by Dr Frank Prendergast.

Below: **At Newgrange passage tomb, Co Meath, monolith GC1 casts a shadow onto the entrance kerbstone at winter solstice sunrise. (Frank Prendergast)**

Slievenamon mountain to the west seen from Knockroe passage tomb.

Chapter 6:

WINTER SOLSTICE AT KNOCKROE, COUNTY KILKENNY

Knockroe passage tomb in southwest County Kilkenny is the only known Irish passage tomb that contains two tombs aligned to two solstice events, to the rising and the setting sun, on the one day.

Known locally as 'The Coshel' (*caiseal*), Knockroe sits in rural landscape above the Lingaun river, a tributary of the important Suir river, in the townland of Knockroe.

Muiris O'Sullivan has directed five seasons of archaeological excavation at Knockroe, which has provided much information about the Neolithic and which prompted the State to buy and conserve the monument.

Knockroe is part of a cluster of passage tombs whose focal point is a cairn on the summit of Slievenamon mountain, 11km to its west. Slievenamon, in Irish *Sliabh na mBan* or Mountain of the Women, is a distinctive mountain in the landscape. It features four megalithic structures: a passage tomb just east of the summit, which is approached on its eastern side by a wide cursus or ceremonial avenue, and two other tombs, one ruined, on its northeastern side.

The summit of Slievenamon is visible from Knockroe and from cist burials at Owen's Hill and Bigg's Lott on Windmill Hill near Cashel.

Tombs at Baunfree, on Kilmacoliver Hill, three kilometres from Knockroe, and at Shrough, near the Glen of Aherlow to the west, are aligned to the summit cairn.

Slievenamon must have been a compelling presence over a wide landscape in the Neolithic era.

Early Neolithic tomb builders appear to have avoided an area of about ten to 15 kilometres around Slievenamon. Extending from the mountain east to the Lingaun river, south to the Suir river and west to the upper, north to south-flowing, stretch of the Suir, no portal tombs or Linkardstown-type mounds have been found in that area, although there are many in other parts of the southeast. They do not seem to go beyond the boundary set by the two rivers. Even recent archaeological investigation along the route of the M9/M10 motorway where they came nearest to Slievenamon found little evidence from the fourth millennium BC.

It appears as if there was some special landscape around Slievenamon that was avoided in the Early Neolithic. Then the passage tombs were built on its summit and the smaller passage tombs were built in a necklace pattern around it. These scattered passage tombs seem to set the limit of an exclusion zone closer to the mountain.

Local antiquarians first brought Knockroe to the attention of archaeologists 30 years ago, when it was virtually unknown. The site was nearly lost to undergrowth, trees,

Below: **The distribution of Neolithic monuments in the Suir valley suggests the area around Slievenamon was avoided by early Neolithic tomb builders. (Frank Prendergast)**

Right above: **Varying sized stones used in the structure of the cairn seen at the west tomb. (Muiris O'Sullivan)**

Right below: **Kerbstones at Knockroe passage tomb before it was excavated. (Muiris O'Sullivan)**

Opposite page: **Knockroe overlooks the Lingaun river with the hills of Baunfree (left) and Carrigadoon (right) and the Comeragh mountains in the distance. (Muiris O'Sullivan)**

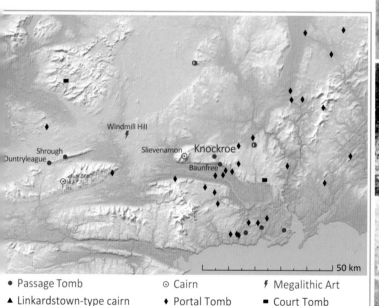

- ● Passage Tomb
- ▲ Linkardstown-type cairn
- ⊙ Cairn
- ◆ Portal Tomb
- ⚡ Megalithic Art
- ■ Court Tomb

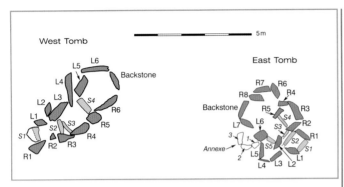

West Tomb

East Tomb

Backstone

Backstone

Annexe

dumped clearance stones and the wear and tear of millennia.

Knockroe passage tomb sits on sloping ground resting on a platform that supports the southern part of the cairn. Within the cairn are two separate passage tombs, east and west, with entrance passages from the southeast and the southwest respectively.

The cairn structure consists of three layers: a base layer of boulders about 30–40cm in size embedded in dark, reddish-purple soil, a middle layer of smaller stones similar to usual cairn fill and an upper layer of small stones that appear to be dumped field clearance. Beneath the cairn are arcs of stones of a kind often found in Middle Neolithic passage tombs and Linkardstown-type mounds.

The cairn is retained behind a megalithic kerb resting against a bank of internal boulders. On the southern side, very large kerbstones form an arc that stretches southeast to southwest between the two entrance areas.

Above: **Plans showing the layout of the west (left) and east (right) tombs at Knockroe. (Muiris O'Sullivan)**

The west tomb has a higher profile than the east, is built from larger stones and its entrance is more imposing. Inside, however, the layout of its internal chamber is simpler than that of the east tomb. The east tomb is lower in height and the internal layout is cruciform in design. The face of the cairn at this direction was decorated originally with quartz. The east tomb may have been part of an earlier cairn with the west tomb added or extended later.

In the east tomb, in the right-hand, north-eastern, recess the flattened remains of part of a Carrowkeel Ware pottery bowl and sherds of other Neolithic pottery were found. The bottom part of the vessel was reconstructed. Like Carrowkeel Ware bowls found at extra-mural cists in the Mound of the Hostages at Tara, this nearly complete vessel may have been left in the recess as a final gesture, perhaps having been used to transport the cremated remains during deposition ceremonies. Between the east tomb and the kerbs fragments of Beaker pottery were found.

In the west tomb, fragments of what may have been a large decorated bone pin, similar to ones found at Knowth and Fourknocks, in County Meath, were found among cremated material. A Food Vessel from the Bronze Age was also found.

Between both tombs but especially the west tomb, the cremated bones of 50–100 people, and occasional pieces of unburnt bone, were found. Some burial deposits seemed to have survived fairly intact especially between the floor stones and between some of the orthostats L1 and L2. Some of the deposits in the east tomb were dense and seemingly undisturbed.

The builders of Knockroe used
many distinctive-looking stones
at selected areas of the tomb.

Knockroe's builders used a large amount of distinctive-looking stones with natural anomalies such as hollows, inclusions or unusual shapes. It is almost as if they had selected stones as if they had a personality of their own. Such stones and the areas of the tomb in which they were used undoubtedly carried symbolic meaning for the builders. Quartzite was used at the tomb entrances; a red sandstone pillar was placed beside the inner sill-stone in the west tomb and a decorated kerb-stone of coarse-grained sandstone was chosen to carry a serpentiform design.

This is just one of a number of links or similarities to the structure of the tombs in the Boyne valley. The Boyne tombs contain the same range and position of stone types, including greywacke, red sandstone, quartz,

Above: **Knowth in the Boyne valley, seen here, and Knockroe both sit above a river that flows east then southwards. (Ken Williams)**

Opposite page: **Sandstone kerbstone decorated with wavy, serpent-like lines. (Muiris O'Sullivan)**

quartzite and water-rolled granite-type stones. There is one significant difference: the raw materials were available within two to three kilometres of Knockroe, whereas the builders in the Boyne valley drew different material from a wide region extending from Wicklow to Louth.

The builders of Knockroe clearly knew their region well and were aware of the outcrops that provided abundant prized or unusual stones, like greywacke, red sandstone and quartz. It may have been the reason why they built Knockroe in that location.

Knockroe also shares with Knowth a particular relationship with the landscape: each sits above a river that is flowing eastward then turns sharply southwards with a fording point.

ALIGNMENTS

Although other passage tombs in the 'necklace' are aligned on the summit of Slievenamon, Knockroe is aligned on the midwinter sun.

Each year, growing numbers of visitors gather at the western tomb to watch the setting sun dip below the western horizon on midwinter day. Solar alignments at the site, observations and technical measurements confirmed that the west tomb is aligned to the point on the horizon where the setting sun dips out of sight shortly after 4pm on 21 December.

During the 2010 excavation, the clearance of collapsed material at the entrance to the west tomb showed that the outer end of the passage was angled slightly but noticeably north of the central axis or the direct setting point of the sun. This changing of the entrance arrangements must have been deliberate and may have been related to the expansion or restructuring of the overall tomb.

Excavations also found that a small triangular boulder, orthostat 3, was less embedded than the other structural stones and could be moved around. The setting sunlight moves around this stone: when looking at it from

(Ken Williams)

Midwinter sunset seen from the west tomb, Knockroe, on 21 December.

98

Artwork at the west tomb.

behind the tomb, it appears to its left before it has reached the horizon and moves to the right of the stone when it reaches the horizon. At Maeshowe tomb in the Orkney islands a moveable stone could be swivelled to block the entrance to the passage and control the entry of light. A similar arrangement was found in the excavation of Newgrange where a stone block resting in the roofbox could be moved around to affect the access of sunlight.

The alignment of the eastern tomb on midwinter sunrise is less well known. The tomb is lower, it does not have an extended passage and because of modern tree growth there is a less easily established solstice line. Sunrise seems to be farther away than the

Above: **Artwork at the east tomb is heavily worn.**

setting sun viewed from the west tomb and the solstice event is less spectacular. However, survey measurements show that the axis of the east tomb is aligned with the midwinter sun rising from behind nearby hills.

It is important to bear in mind that the alignment of a tomb structure on a rising or setting sun at certain times of the year is designed to refer not just to the time of the year but also to the local topography. The precise point at which the rising or setting sun apparently crosses the horizon on midwinter day is subject to the closeness or height of the skyline as seen from that site. At Knockroe the sun appears to set much closer on the western side and the ground is high, whereas sunrise viewed at the east tomb seems much farther away. It is a uniquely local phenomenon at every site and would have needed prior knowledge to predict its occurrence and to locate the tomb in line with it.

STONE ART

Knockroe is exceptional for the amount and sophistication of megalithic art that adorns its structural stones. Thirty-five decorated stones have been found though, in the case of some, the art has been worn greatly by weather erosion. Some of the designs in the west tomb are comparable to the superb art found in the Boyne valley tombs or in Brittany. Again, differences can be seen between the two tombs. Artwork in the east tomb is relatively small-scale, lightly-picked oval designs, which has been heavily worn, while stones lining the passage of the west tomb carry spirals, cupmarks and zig-zag designs. The arc of kerbstones bounding the southern part of the tomb contains decorated slabs, one of them displaying rows of serpent-like lines, while the northern side of the kerb carries no artwork other than two opposing, very small arc shapes on one kerbstone.

The location of megalithic art, the placement of different types of stones and the focus on the sun are interlinked. The arc of decorated kerbstones stretching from southeast to southwest along the cairn's face reflects the apparent journey of the midwinter sun from sunrise to sunset. The single kerbstone at the northern area of the cairn that bears the two, small arc shapes is the stone through which the solstice axis extends. The absence of art also may acknowledge the absence of the sun's light at that point. The use of quartz around the tomb entrances and the incorporation of a red sandstone pillar in the western tomb on the line of the main solstice orientation were a deliberate use of symbolism, perhaps bound

up in their colour. It echoes the use of different coloured stones in megalithic structures in Scotland.

Emphasis on the solar alignment of many passage graves may blind us to other elements of their design that may give insights into the thinking of their builders. We can use the monuments to glimpse aspects of the mythology, in the sense of the explanation of the world view, of people in ancient times, how their society understood the world, how it dealt with existential questions, what their beliefs and knowledge might have been and how their ideas about these things were reflected in art and architecture.

The axis line of solar alignment may serve to divide the interior of a tomb into separate and opposite halves and not just in those cairns that contain two opposite-facing tombs. At Newgrange passage grave, the solar axis divides the tomb and cairn in two. As if to act as a permanent reminder of the internal division, the decoration on the stones at the front and at the rear of the cairn, K1 and K52, is divided by a central line down the middle of the design. The central line on K52 has a channel that acts as a border between separate design fields and the central line on K1 is almost lost among swirling spirals. The external lines seem to reflect the division of the space within.

At Knowth tomb, the dividing axis is reflected by a central line on the entrance stone in front of both tombs. The profusion of decorated kerbstones at Knowth raises questions about the smaller and undecorated kerbstones near satellite 13 and likewise the absence of decorated kerbstones along the northern perimeter at Knockroe. These features, too, might reflect the division of the tomb into separate zones.

Therefore, the axis of orientation is not just a function of an external orientation to the sun or a point on the landscape but also of the division of the monument itself into opposite halves. These opposites are not just north and south but also right and left, as is seen in many cruciform passage tombs, including the cruciform chambers of Newgrange, Knowth and Knockroe.

Right and left are opposites used by many societies as symbols to refer to things beyond themselves. Left is associated with all negative connotations. The Latin word 'sinister', which transferred into the English language means starting from the left or unfavourable. The Irish word for left, *tuathalach,* means awkward, difficult, anti-clockwise or against the sun.

Many other cultures use right and left to distinguish between preferred and undesirable qualities. In the biblical scene of the Last Judgment on the 9th–10th century Muiredach's high cross at Monasterboice in County Louth or the same scene by Michelangelo in the Sistine Chapel in Rome, the damned are on Christ's left. Gospel accounts of the crucifixion of Christ put the bad thief on the cross to Christ's left. In Irish passage tombs the right-hand cell is nearly always more elaborate than the left.

Sun, light, left, right are recurring symbols in human society. Polarization is a method used by society to understand the world and frame a world view relating to concepts of good and evil, day and night, life and death, heaven and hell. Though the real world is more complex than polarized images suggest, the symbolic scales are important points of

Above: **Scene of the Last Judgment carved on Muiredach's high cross at Monasterboice, Co Louth. (Ken Williams)**

Opposite page: **A central line divides artwork on kerbstone 52 at Newgrange. (Ken Williams)**

reference for society. We cannot assume that the mythology of these tomb builders was shallow or one dimensional. They were probably just as sophisticated in this area as in any other.

Sun and light are other symbols used to represent ideas about the world or society. The sun or sunlight have been used throughout history to represent influential ideas and ideals, for example, the opening words of Genesis in the Bible — 'and God said let there be light; and there was light'[1] — or the term Enlightenment for the scientific advances of 18th century Europe.

The moon, too, symbolizes certain understood references.

Ideas about light and its symbolism have been reflected in art and architecture in many cultures or times. The cathedral of San Lorenzo in Turin, Italy, and the royal chapel-mosque Masjed-e Šayk Lotf-Allāh in Isfahan, Iran, both built in the 17th century but reflecting different religions and cultures, embed in their structures ideas about light and its symbolism. These, in turn, define how people experienced the buildings and their interiors and had their world views reinforced. The design of these buildings combined several disciplines from science and mathematics to theology. The same thing might be said about Newgrange, Knockroe or Cairn T at Loughcrew.

In Ireland, only a minority of passage tombs are oriented at astronomical phenomena. A significant number are oriented to other cairns often on mountain tops. Some have no apparent rationale for their orientation. If movements of the sun are seen as the primary purpose for the orientation of Irish passage tombs, how can those tombs without obvious alignment or orientation be explained?

These symbols and metaphors offer the most promising line of explanation for the interest of passage tombs in the sun. While we continually seek to understand what solar events meant to passage tomb society at winter or summer solstice, we view it through the lens of our individual, personal beliefs, backgrounds and knowledge of passage tomb society. That modern experience is equally valid so long as we realize that those experiences tell us more about ourselves than they do about passage tomb society.

●

Adapted by Peigín Doyle from the conference presentation by Professor Muiris O'Sullivan.

Below: **Light and shadow in the prayer hall in the Sheikh Lotf-Allāh mosque in Isfahan, Iran. (Sadegh Panahi)**

Opposite page: **Decorated kerbstone in moonlight. The moon symbolised ideas about the cosmos. (Ken Williams)**

[1.] King James Bible, Genesis, Chapter 1.

Solstice sunlight lights up the chamber of Newgrange passage grave.

Chapter 7:

ART, ARCHITECTURE AND ASTRONOMY IN THE IRISH PASSAGE TOMB TRADITION

At the winter solstice sunrise at Newgrange, as the beam of light illuminates the floor of the tomb, a person would need to be lying on the floor with their face on the ground to see anything outside the tomb through the window of viewing. That is the experience of researcher and photographer Ken Williams who has worked for 15 years to photograph every known or possible solar alignment across Ireland.

In passage graves, we tend to describe alignments as a view taken along a fixed straight line drawn from the axis of the passage or chamber and extended to the horizon or sky outside. Rather, it is the movement of the sun's beam across the floor and the chamber stones within the tomb that is crucial to the experience and the symbolism being expressed in solar alignments, according to Williams.

Solar phenomena offer a diverse range of aesthetic experiences and many are compelling witness to the changing of the seasons and the turning of the year. Stone circles seem designed to draw the eye upwards to view the setting sun on the horizon whereas passage tombs show a particular concern with drawing the gaze inward, metaphorically as much as physically. The emotional experience of such symbolic events is difficult to fully convey in a numerical chart or diagram.

Debate about passage tombs is often couched as a question of whether they are

Above: **Stone circles seem to draw the eye towards the sun on the horizon. (Ken Williams)**

temples, calendars or tombs. Rather than being in opposition, the potency of the tomb draws on all three functions but the dead are of central importance.

When excavated, Irish passage tombs typically have been found to contain cremated and unburnt human bone, in the passages, the chambers, in basins and beneath and behind structural stones. The tomb may not have been the first resting place of these dead people. In the case of some, it may not have been their final destination.

The discovery in the great tomb at Knowth of artefacts still encrusted with the cremated ashes among which they had been placed had the power to be deeply moving. A televised re-enactment of a cremation ritual at Knowth, in which Williams took part, which used an animal as stand-in for a person, with all the sounds and sights of the dark night and with the shadow of the tomb looming behind, gave an unforgettable sense of how it might have felt to be there at the original rituals in the Neolithic. Such experience led Williams to believe that a solar event witnessed by a solitary individual within the tomb was incomplete, without the crowds gathered to witness and celebrate the spectacle as he believes it was intended.

NEWGRANGE

The observation of the rising solstice sun at Newgrange passage tomb at Brú na Bóinne, by archaeologist Michael O'Kelly, in winter 1967 was a significant moment in modern archaeoastronomy. The passage of the tomb was found to face directly to the point on the horizon where the winter solstice sun rose around 3200 BC, when it was built. The evi-

dence was so strong it was concluded that the alignment was deliberate.

Newgrange passage grave, the pre-eminent tomb in a ritual landscape of over 40 tombs and related structures extending along an elevated ridge above the river Boyne, was built on sloping land and constructed in three stages with the original tomb being extended in size over time. At its final, finished size, the length and angle of the sloping passage would have prevented the sun's rays from reaching the back chamber of the tomb.

Above: **A Beaker pot and remains of cremated bone deposited in Knowth. (Ken Williams)**

Decorated stone basin in the right recess of the eastern tomb at Knowth.

(Ken Williams)

An ingenious feature, the roofbox, was built above and behind the entrance to admit the light, not through the main entrance but directly above it. This elaborate device was termed the roofbox by its excavator Michael O'Kelly. From within the chamber, the roofbox, which is overhead when entering the tomb, is at floor level due to the rising passage. Nevertheless, light pouring through the roofbox at winter solstice sunrise illuminates the floor of the chamber 19 metres or 60 feet within the interior of the mound, despite the upward slope of the passage and even when the massive door-slab sealing the tomb is in position.

By the time excavation commenced at Newgrange in 1962, the exterior and passage of the monument were suffering the effects of thousands of years of natural weathering and the efforts of amateurs or early archaeologists to investigate the mound. Many of the orthostats were leaning into the outer

Above: **Recreation of a Neolithic cremation ritual in the shadow of Knowth. (Ken Williams)**

Winter solstice sunlight lights up the floor of the chamber deep within the interior of the tomb.

Above: Solstice sunrise seen from Newgrange passage grave. (Ken Williams)

(Ken Williams)

passage and some had to be supported by wooden blocks. Some of the Neolithic artwork was being worn by the numbers of people rubbing against it as they crawled beneath the orthostats to enter the chamber. As part of conservation work, the covering cairn and the roof slabs of the passage were removed to stabilize and re-set the leaning orthostats. It was during this work that the roofbox, and the decorated lintel projecting above, were uncovered.

When examined, it was found to be a funnel-shaped structure, its sides consisting of low-drystone walls capped by a roofstone on each wall, the top made of overlapping slabs and the rear closed by the front edge of the second roofstone.

Two large upright stones create a gap between the top of the first roofstone and the bottom of the second and through this crucial opening the light of the rising sun pours on winter solstice morning.

The presence of the roofbox allows the solstice phenomenon to occur. It points persuasively to the special importance the solstice sun held for Ireland's Neolithic peoples. Williams suggests, further, that the upward angle of the floor inside was structured so that the light could be seen retreating back

Above: **The roofbox at Newgrange in the process of excavation. The quartz block can be seen clearly at back left. (Ken Williams)**

Left: **The Newgrange roofbox created by the gap between the top of roofstone 1 and the bottom of roofstone 2. (Ken Williams)**

Opposite page: **People witness winter solstice sunrise at Dowth passage tomb. (Ken Williams)**

down the passageway.

In addition to the tomb's abundant megalithic art, the roofbox is one of the defining features of Newgrange, making it one of a small number of Neolithic structures of global note and designated, since 1993, a UNESCO World Heritage site.

When first excavated, archaeologist M.J. O'Kelly recorded that a quartz block was found in the roof gap and had signs of having been moved repeatedly to allow light into the chamber, in an example of active direction of the light that has been suggested at tombs in the Orkneys and at Knockroe, County

Kilkenny. It would have been moved also to seal the roofbox during the periods between winter solstices.

A vivid description of the quartz block provided by archaeologist Frances Lynch gave its dimensions as 25–30 cm long, about 20 cm in cross section, angular in shape with abraded corners and larger than the gap behind it so it could not have fallen through the gap but had originally been located where it was found in the roofbox.

Williams sees the evidence of a block being moved frequently to admit light to the space within as proof that the solstice experience was not just a passive occasion but something in which people were actively engaged.

Professor O'Kelly also had suggested that scratch marks on the top rear surface of the first roof slab showed that a second block might have been originally in place, although such a block was not found during excavations and may have been disturbed by unqualified interference in the past.

When conservation work was carried out on the tomb after excavation, the roofslabs, lintel and surrounding stones were reinstated in their original recorded positions. The accuracy of the reconstruction was achieved through the detailed and meticulous excavation record, amplified by precise scale drawings and a large array of photographs. This material was presented in O'Kelly's 1982 main excavation report, *Newgrange: Archaeology, Art and Legend,* and in an extensive collection of records and photographs that he deposited, along with his personal archive, in the Irish National Monuments archives.

However, at some point in time the quartz block appeared to have gone missing and there was no modern record or photographs of its whereabouts. Its absence prompted some commentators to suggest that the roofbox had been constructed or altered during conservation work and was not an original feature of the Neolithic structure.

Having searched O'Kelly's excavation archive and the National Monuments

Below: **An example of the rich linear-style artwork at Knowth. (Ken Williams)**

The decorated stone, Orthostat 49, in the western tomb at Knowth.

Photographic Records Office, Williams found two photographs that showed the quartz block in place where Professor O'Kelly had described it. The stone seen in the photographs was confirmed by expert Frances Lynch as the original quartz block.

The photographs are an invaluable record of the state of the roofbox at the time of exca- vation and of the emphasis placed on return- ing it to its original position in the structure when restoration work was carried out.

In the same photographs, roofstone 2 is leaning heavily to the east where it had sunken downwards. The western end was originally high up above roofstone 1 leaving a small gap in between. Roofing corbels had

also dropped below the level of roofstone 1. When the corbels were raised into their original positions as part of conservation, the size of the roofbox gap was restored to how it had been when first built.

Above: **Art motifs in Newgrange carved on structural stones where they cannot be seen. (Ken Williams)**

Opposite page: **Kerbstone No. 15 at Knowth displays an array of megalithic art motifs. (Ken Williams)**

The reinstatement of the roofbox and roof-stones renewed one of the most ancient, spectacular and moving displays of prehistoric archaeology, which combines engineering, artistry, drama and spirituality like few other constructions before or since.

MEGALITHIC ART

The meaning of motifs and symbols adorning the structural stones of many passage tombs is still unknown, though many theories, ranging from astronomy to the marine, have been put forward. While Neolithic art in the form of pottery and small grave goods is found in the two western European passage grave regions of the Baltic and the Atlantic coast, only in passage graves of Europe's Atlantic coast is artwork found applied to the structural stones of the tomb itself. Such artwork is referred to as megalithic art and it is particularly abundant and accomplished in the tombs at Brú na Bóinne.

The art of passage tombs takes many distinct forms and all aspects were important within the tombs. Megalithic art found in Irish passage graves is either angular in shape, with zigzags, triangles and diamond-shaped lozenges, or curved in motifs such as spirals, ovals and circles. It blends a distinctive Irish style with motifs found also in Brittany and Iberia. Different styles and symbols are found within different tombs at Brú na Bóinne: spirals and lozenges occur more frequently on the Newgrange tomb while a more linear style is found at Knowth and has parallels in Brittany.

The style of motifs, and the techniques for making them, were applied at different times, starting with incised angular designs followed later by broad lines and then areas of close picking, applied with a stone punch, to create shapes such as lozenges. The spiral motif is an early art style and is rarely found outside Ireland.

Some symbols seem to suggest definite shapes like the sun, moon, stars, objects or concrete events. The decorated stone, ortho-stat 49, within the western tomb of the large passage grave at Knowth, with its confident, abstract design, has been interpreted often as a kind of guardian stone warning those who entered the passage that the burial chamber was just ahead. A similar style of artwork has been found at sites in southern Spain and Portugal. At Newgrange, art on the entrance stones seems to have been expertly carved to impress when seen from a respectful distance.

Some art appears to have been created without any agenda or communication purpose. Some is even hidden where it never would have been seen, on corbels or at the back and the top of structural stones. It has been suggested that some shapes were outlines to guide later painting. To us they are a language that is still unreadable.

Although abstract in design, and in a language we cannot understand, megalithic artwork undoubtedly expresses the beliefs of its creators about life and death and their place within the wider cosmos, as they understood it.

A photographer attempting to record solar events would value the chance of doing so in an empty tomb, to better capture the effect of light on stone as probably it was intended originally. Having photographed these solar occurrences many times, Williams eventually concluded that the event was incomplete

without the presence of people to celebrate or witness the spectacle. Rather than seeing passage grave alignments as forms of agricul-tural, engineering or astronomical technology, they were primarily an expression of social technology right from the very first communal gathering of building stones.

●

Adapted by Peigín Doyle from the conference presentation by Ken Williams.

Above: **Summer solstice sunrise on the horizon seem from Townleyhall passage grave, Co Louth. (Ken Williams)**

Chapter 8:

CULTURAL ASTRONOMY AND CULTURAL HERITAGE: A GLOBAL PERSPECTIVE

All over western Europe, groups of megalithic structures have evident patterns of orientation: some face sunrise, others face sunset and yet others face prominent features in the landscape.

The many varied patterns of orientation found in different ancient societies raise the question of whether archaeoastronomy, which looks to the sky to explain orientation and meaning for structures, is a useful tool for understanding some aspects of ancient peoples' beliefs and ways of living.

Clive Ruggles has studied what has become known as 'cultural astronomy' in prehistoric Europe, Polynesia, pre-Columbian America and Africa. His work has convinced him that if we are to seek to know what people in the past thought about the cosmos and the sky, we need to have a much wider interest in all their practices and beliefs.

Western culture has developed a way of classifying what we observe in the 'natural world' into separate, distinct categories, which we study using various scientific disciplines such as botany, biology, geology and so on. This reflects the system of categorizing organisms and minerals devised by the 18th century Swedish botanist Carl Linnaeus. In this way of looking at things, 'If it is in the sky (and above the clouds) then it is astronomy'.

Archaeoastronomers in Europe often have adopted a data-driven approach to the study of megalithic structures, undertaking first-hand surveys and using statistical tools to establish local or regional patterns of orientation. Despite its limitations, this type of approach has produced some huge steps forward in our understanding of certain groups of megalithic structures. Michael Hoskin, for example, surveyed 177 seven-stone *antas* (dolmens) in central Portugal and Spain and showed that every one faced sunrise at some date during the year, mostly in autumn, spring or winter. They were all built during the fourth millennium BC and provide the oldest statistically demonstrable evidence of a group of monuments aligned to sunrise at different times of the year.

Hoskin's broader research, based on surveys of over 3000 later prehistoric tombs in western Europe and the Mediterranean, showed that there were different local patterns of orientation but clearly demonstrated overall that orientation with respect to the sun was of wide importance, if different from place to place and time to time, and needed to be taken into account when studying different groups of monuments. That said, other aspects of landscape can also help explain the orientation of tombs, a prominent example being Menga, one of three huge Iberian dolmens at Antequera in Spain, which faces a mountain whose shape resembles the head of a person lying down with their face upwards.

Other cultures understand their universe by making links across our Linnaean boundaries. They see meaning in various connections that they notice and this includes what they perceive in the sky. Perceptions of the sky are not something apart; they form an integral part of their broader understanding of the

cosmos, life, death, and the cycles of nature.

Archaeoastronomy is important because, while we know very little about the appearance of the actual environment or landscape in ancient times, we do know exactly what the configurations of the sun, moon, stars and planets looked like to people in the past. However, we need to explain the orientation of megalithic structures from their perspective. Using the term 'observatory' implies that a site was built primarily, or even exclusively, for observing the stars. The term is obviously inappropriate in the case of astronomically

Above: **British archaeoastronomer Michael Hoskin standing by Anta de la Marquesa (Mellizo), Valencia de Alcántara, Spain, one of the seven-stone antas that are all aligned upon sunrise. (© Clive Ruggles)**

Opposite page: **A string of dark patches obscuring the bright Milky Way were identified by aboriginal Australians as a giant celestial emu. Pictured here in Victoria, Australia, it stretches down from the dark Coalsack nebula (its head) to the horizon, where the moon and some bright planets are also seen. (NASA/Alex Cherney, Terrastro, TWAN)**

The Governor's Palace, Uxmal, Mexico, aligned to the rising and setting of Venus in the year it was built.

oriented tombs but it is best avoided also in the case of other types of site. Ruggles argues for a balanced approach between the scientific and the cultural to see where astronomy fits into wider questions of society and belief.

Unlike European prehistorians, archaeologists in parts of the world such as in Latin America, studying more recent archaeological remains, are able to draw upon a broader range of sources to throw light on the meaning of astronomical orientations, such as history, ethnography and records left by early European colonizers. This leads them to insights and conclusions that could not be reached through the archaeological evidence alone.

THE MAYA

Evidence from the Mayan culture of Mexico and Central America provides various practical examples of the limitations of a purely data-driven approach. The Maya kept extremely long calendars: their cyclical calendar only repeated after a 52-year 'calendar round' and they also had a 'long count' that progressed linearly. They often inscribed the long count date on buildings at the time of their construction. Knowledge of their calendars and related practices allows archaeologists to identify and interpret Mayan structural orientations in a way that could not be done by simply analyzing the structure.

One of the clearest examples occurs at the Mayan city of Uxmal in Mexico's Yucatan Peninsula, at the so-called Governor's Palace, a building dating from around AD 900. This is aligned differently from other buildings at the site and upon another pyramid called Cehtzuc. The alignment also matches the

most northerly setting of the planet Venus around the year, which is determinable from its long count date. Since the alignment is a one-off and Venus' extreme positions vary from one cycle to the next, the possible significance of the orientation would be impossible to establish if it were not for the inscribed date.

The evidence available from building inscriptions and historical documents also enables us to confirm the intentionality of the alignment and to suggest some aspects of its cultural significance. Hieroglyphic inscriptions carved on the front of the building contain many references to Venus. To a

Above: **Carved image of the Mesoamerican god Quetzalcoatl from the Temple of Quetzalcoatl at Teotihuacan, Mexico.** (© Clive Ruggles)

Opposite page: **The north face of the Temple of Masks, a stepped pyramid that was part of the Group E complex at the Mayan city of Uaxactun.** (David Germain, CC-BY-SA-2.5)

Mayan the building was clearly flagged as relating to Venus.

Rather than simply examining the physical site and identifying possible targets for orientation, archaeologists can examine Mayan sources to see what features in the sky were important to them. The Mayans kept detailed astronomical tables recording the movements of Venus and the moon over long periods. They record, among other things, that the most northerly point at which Venus appears in the evening sky happens in the rainy season of April and May, which would be a significant time for agriculture. Because the appearance of Venus in the sky heralded the rainy season, it was associated with the Mesoamerican god Quetzalcoatl, the feathered serpent, who was related to rain, maize and fertility.

GROUP E STRUCTURES

Group E structures is the name given to a characteristic formation of buildings found at many Mayan ceremonial sites in northern Guatemala.

Uaxactun was a major Mayan city and one of the longest occupied, dating back to 300 BC or earlier. It was the first Mayan site to be excavated by archaeologists in the region and included the Group E complex whose name came to be adopted more generally. The formation consisted of a main stepped pyramid on the western side facing a rectangular platform, elongated from north to south, typically with two or (as at Uaxactun itself) three smaller pyramid-shaped structures on its top.

Viewed from the east-facing staircase of the western pyramid, the rising sun at the summer and winter solstices appeared in line with the outer edges of the northernmost and southernmost platform-top structures, respectively, while at the equinoxes it rose above the central one. Based on these solar alignments, the Group E structures at Uaxactun were assumed to have been built for astronomical purposes.

However, as similar formations started to be discovered at other sites, it became increasingly obvious that, despite similarities in their layout and orientation, few if any duplicated the accurate solar alignments found at Uaxactun. Furthermore, the archaeological evidence shows that over time the Group E formation at Uaxactun itself was elaborated, in accordance with the Mayan practice of building a new structure on top of an existing one when a new calendar cycle commenced, so that the original solar alignments no longer functioned. One interpretation is that in these later stages of development, as found at many other sites, the connection with the sun was already established and did not need to be reinforced by direct observation. These settings had become symbolic rather than functional in marking the sun.

Group E structures are now believed to be ceremonial spaces where ideas relating to time, agricultural cycles and power as part of the cosmic order were acted out in symbolic, communal rituals.

HAWAI'I

The Hawaiian Islands stretch in a chain of eight major islands plus atolls and smaller isles across some 2400 kilometres of the north Pacific. Now a state of the United States, the

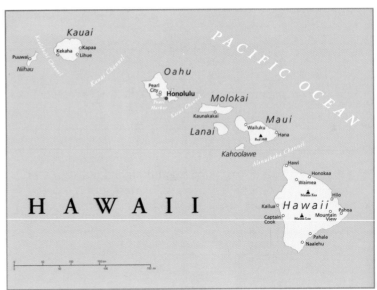

archipelago was originally settled by Polynesian people voyaging north from Tahiti in around AD 1000. Polynesians knew a great deal about the heavens and navigated the Pacific guided by stars. As the Hawaiian population grew, people gradually spread out from agriculturally productive wetland areas into the harsher dryland environments of the eastern, volcanically younger, islands. One of the harshest was the region of Kahikinui, in the south of the island of Maui.

When Captain James Cook arrived towards the end of the 18th century, Hawaiian society was centred around a strict social order and set of taboos, the *kapu* system, sustained by high chiefs (kings) and priests.

Temples called *heiau* were sacred spaces used for worship and sacrifice. They varied in size from large royal temples to simple fishing shrines, and served many different functions from healing the sick to controlling the rain or securing victory in war. They were also dedicated to different gods.

Heiau generally were built of rough volcanic stone (*'a-ā*). Some were platforms; others were enclosures. They could be rectangular in form or square, L-shaped, or more irregular and they could be sited on hills, on low ground, in valleys or on the coast. Upon the larger stone platforms once stood thatched buildings, sometimes to house a priest, wooden towers, altars, offering stands and carved images of gods.

Maui is the second largest, and second most easterly, of the large Hawaiian Islands.

Pacific Ocean

0 1.5 3   6   9   12   15 Kilometers

Above right: **Map of Kahikinui district, the arid southern area of Maui where about 70 *heiau* have been found. (© Patrick V. Kirch)**

Below: **Engraving of a royal *heiau* at Tiritatea Bay in 1816 by Jean-Pierre Norblin de La Gourdaine. (Creative Commons)**

Opposite page: **The principal islands of the Hawaiian chain in the Pacific. (Shutterstock)**

The arid backlands of Kahikinui have remained relatively untouched by the influx of European settlers since the nineteenth century. Together with the adjacent region of Kaupō, Kahikinui contains about 70 documented *heiau*.

Pieces of branch coral often were placed as offerings on altars and inserted in the wall stones during construction. Because the corals are organic, they have enabled many of the Kahikinui *heiau* to be accurately dated. The analysis of coral samples from 26 temple sites shows that the Kahikinui *heiau* mostly were built over a period between AD 1550 and 1700. The great majority were built over a period of 50–60 years, with eight inland temples being dated to between 1572 and 1603.

A data-driven approach reveals patterns in the principal orientation, or *kapu* direction, of the Kahikinui *heiau*. There is a group broadly facing east, another north-facing group, a tight group facing east-northeast, and, finally, a number of coastal *heiau* that face out to sea. But this only gets us so far.

We can understand more about the orientations of the *heiau* by considering accounts by early Hawaiian authors, which tell us a great deal about Hawaiian history, culture, ideology and the evolution of Hawaiian society.

Early Hawaiian religion was animistic and concerned with the natural forces of the tides, sky, volcanic activity and nature. The chief gods worshipped by the Hawaiians were Kū, Kāne, Lono, and Kanaloa, together with many lesser gods, some associated with certain occupations, and guardian spirits of particular families. Kū was the god of war but was associated also with the colour red and the direction north; Kāne embodied the male power of procreation and also was associated with the sun and the east; Lono was the god of dryland agriculture, birth and fertility; and Kanaloa was associated with death, the subterranean world and the ocean.

We can see now that each type of temple is associated with one of the chief gods. The northerly group of temples face a ridge of the Haleakalā volcano, in several cases pointing particularly at red cinder cones in the landscape. They are clearly Kū temples and oriented topographically. The easterly-facing *heiau* face the rising sun and are presumably associated with Kāne. The coastal temples associated with Kanaloa are simply oriented in relation to their coastal position and the direction of the sea.

That leaves the east-northeast-facing temples, concentrated in upland areas where rainfall supported crops and most people lived

The Pleiades star cluster, sometimes called The Seven Sisters, is found in the modern constellation of Taurus the Bull. They form a distinctive feature in the night sky in both the northern and southern hemispheres and were known and recorded in cultures around the world. The name comes from Ancient Greek and may well derive from the word *plein*, to sail, given the stars' importance in heralding the sailing season in the Mediterranean.

The Nebra sky disc, a decorated Bronze- or Iron- Age disc from Northern Germany, features a cluster of dots that some believe to be the earliest known representation of the Pleiades.

Below: **The bronze and gold Nebra sky disc where seven dots have been suggested to represent the Pleiades. (© Amanda Chadburn)**

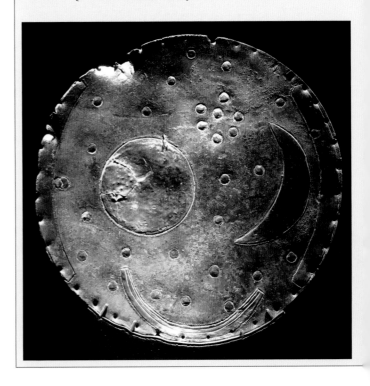

THE PLEIADES

The Hawaiians' called the Pleiades *Makaliʻi*.

In Hawaiʻi, the first appearance of the Pleiades at sunset marked the beginning of the Mahahiki season, a time when wars ceased and chiefs (who were perceived as gods) exercised and reinforced their power by making ritualized circuits around the country exacting tributes.

Hawaiian society was based on agricultural production. Access to surplus food would give a chief the resources to support warriors and to enhance his political and economic power. Rulers increased their religious authority by building temples. By building a Lono temple near agricultural land a chief could associate himself with the harvest and the gods and create a case for food tributes from the population. This was reinforced by linking the associated rituals to the calendar by making the temple itself an observation point for the Pleiades.

The building of *heiau* was also related to political developments in Maui. Early society in the Hawaiian Islands had been organized into a number of small chiefdoms. Over time a centralized monarchy developed. The short period of 150 years when most of the Maui *heiau* were built coincided with oral records of the creation of a centralized kingdom under kings Piʻilani, Kia-a-Piʻilani and Kamalalawalu. Recognizing the astronomical associations of some of the temples helps us to understand this process of transformation.

This example shows how astronomy forms part, but by no means all, of the picture as regards Hawaiian temple orientations. Astronomy operated in a broader cultural context. The example also shows how studying archaeoastronomy can help us to investigate broader social questions of interest to all archaeologists.

Above: **A typical Kahikinui temple (*heiau*), NAK-30, in its landscape setting. (© Clive Ruggles)**

Temple (*heiau*) ALE-140 in Kahikinui, Maui, with Clive Ruggles undertaking a theodolite survey.

and farmed. These were Lono *heiau*, relating to agriculture and the seasonal calendar. They face roughly towards the June solstice sunrise but that is not the intended astronomical target. They point to the rising of the Pleiades star group. The first appearance of the Pleiades before dawn and at sunset were events that divided the calendrical year throughout Polynesia. In fact, a number of these Lono temples incorporate sighting devices. In one case a small lava pillar was placed next to a natural stone 300m away from the *heiau* so as to form a 'gunsight' framing the rising Pleiades.

NAZCA, PERU

It is unwise to be preoccupied exclusively with finding astronomical functions for stone structures. It can be deeply misleading also to jump to defining them as observatories if they show orientation to heavenly bodies. The Nazca 'geoglyphs' are a large group of geometric figures and lines created over a wide area of the Nazca desert in southern Peru between 100 BC and AD 700 by brushing aside small stones on the surface to reveal the soft sand beneath. They include world-famous stylized depictions of animals such as a jaguar, monkey and hummingbird, but also a huge network of straight lines, radial 'line centres', and wide trapezoids. They have baffled scholars since the 1920s with many theories advanced for their purpose, both scholarly and outlandish, including ideas that they were walkways for gods, pilgrim paths, irrigation systems, or extra-terrestrial landing sites. The theory that they had an astronomical purpose has gained widespread popular notoriety.

One huge labyrinth, discovered by Ruggles in 1984 and mapped 20 years later, seems to have been intended to be walked but its excellent condition suggests also that it never was walked by more than a few people. It makes no sense as a 'figure' seen from the air and no part of it appears to have been astronomically oriented.

A recent, five-year intensive study of the Nazca geoglyphs found little clear evidence of any astronomical intent. It is true that a handful of straight lines are solstitially aligned but this is no more than would be expected by chance. The geoglyphs most likely had a variety of purposes. Some, evidently, were to be walked. An overriding preoccupation was water and many geoglyphs clearly relate to people's never-ending efforts to convince the gods to send rains down from the mountains.

We only have a few tantalizing strands of evidence that relate to people's perceptions in the past. We cannot be sure what they saw when they looked at the landscape around them and we have no idea what they imagined to be there. But we know what they saw when they looked at the stars; we know where on the horizon the astronomical bodies rose and set for them. The sky is the one part of prehistoric people's environment that we can, in effect, 'see' for ourselves by using modern astronomy and winding the clock back.

There are many different reasons why people might have oriented their structures in the way they did and some of these we will never be able to know. But where an alignment related to what people saw in the sky, we have the potential to discover that fact, although, of course, we must recognize that the mere existence of an astronomical alignment does not, in itself, prove that it was intentional.

Interpretation of the cultural significance of an astronomically oriented structure is much trickier. The solstitial alignment of Newgrange passage tomb, for example, tells us that a connection existed in the builders' minds between, on the one hand, death, ancestors and ancestral spirits and, on the other, the sun, seasonality and seasonal renewal. But it tells us little more.

Other cultures did not use our Linnaean categories to give structure to their lifeworld. For them, what they saw in the sky was connected to other aspects of their experience in ways largely lost to us. Even where historical sources give us some insights into a past world-view, we must avoid the temptation to leave out the bits that do not seem to make sense to our way of thinking. The tendency is to accept aspects of ancient practice or culture when it seems to accord with our rational, scientific view of things; other aspects we reject as superstition.

The Greek poet Hesiod is a great example of this. Ancient Greek farmers watched star movements to know when to undertake particular types of agricultural work. In the *Works* part of his epic poem *Works and Days*, Hesiod explained in detail for his audience around 700 BC how to use the stars to identify the right time of year for sowing, ploughing and

harvesting. The time for harvest, for example, was when the Pleiades were first seen in the pre-dawn sky. This makes sense to us because we can calculate the time of year of the appearance and disappearance of the Pleiades in different locations and at different epochs and we can see that the seasonal correlations make sense. The *Works* are widely quoted.

On the other hand, the *Days* part is often ignored as it contains advice on which days of the moon (days within a month, counted by lunar phases) are to be favoured or avoided, for example, when shearing sheep or having children of a given gender. This we would dismiss as nothing more than superstition.

We cannot try to understand the world-view of ancient people if we do not consider also the parts that seem irrational to us, because that world-view represents another rationality. Where astronomy is concerned, we always need to be examining wider cultural questions in order to see where the astronomy fits into broader frameworks of understanding.

Archaeoastronomers continue to try to find ways to successfully merge different approaches to studying astronomical orientations and their cultural meaning. The example of the *heiau* (temples) on Maui, which links ideology, agriculture, calendar, astronomy and the emergence of a proto-state, shows how investigating astronomical alignments, as just one part of broader archaeological and historical investigations, can throw light on fundamental social questions.

These *heiau* sites also illustrate why it is important not to ignore potential astronomical connections, nor to concentrate exclusively upon them, where, as in the case of prehistoric

European monuments, we have only the archaeological evidence to go on. They exemplify not only some of the possible reasons for orientation in European and Irish passage tombs other than solar alignments but also demonstrate how cultural astronomy fits into the wider field of archaeology.

Above: **A bottle painted with a crayfish image; an example of pottery produced by the early Nazca culture. (American Museum of Natural History, Creative Commons)**

Opposite page: **Aerial view of part of the Nazca pampa, showing the monkey figure and parallel lines. (© Clive Ruggles)**

Despite huge gaps in time, one of the fundamental things we share with the world's ancestors is the sky. In all societies over time the sky has been an integral and important part of the cosmos, however diversely different cultures might have perceived it.

Astronomy is a central part of the cultural heritage of humanity and knowledge of this heritage enriches us all.

UNESCO, the United Nations Educational, Scientific and Cultural Organization, seeks to build world peace by promoting international co-operation through education, science and culture. Its activities include securing international co-operation to protect the world's cultural and natural heritage. UNESCO's World Heritage List now contains more than 1100 World Heritage Properties (both sites and cultural landscapes).

ASTRONOMY AND WORLD HERITAGE

UNESCO, in partnership with the International Astronomical Union, has promoted a thematic initiative on Astronomy and World Heritage aimed at acknowledging the cultural and scientific values of places connected with astronomy and their role within human culture.

The potential scope of this initiative is huge, ranging from ancient monuments to classical and modern observatories and even including the heritage of space exploration. Stonehenge was inscribed onto the World Heritage List as early as 1986 but it was not until 2008 that the solstitial alignments at Stonehenge and nearby contemporary sites within the World Heritage Property were recognized by UNESCO as part of its 'outstanding universal value'.

www.whc.unesco.org/en/astronomy (UNESCO Astronomy and World Heritage Thematic Initiative)

www.astronomicalheritage.net (UNESCO portal to the heritage of astronomy)

www.iau.org (International Astronomical Union)

Opposite page: **Absence of light pollution at Knowth reveals the beauty of the night sky. (Ken Williams)**

Right: **The thirteen towers of Chankillo, an astronomical heritage site in Peru. The towers form part of a solar observation device built around 220 BC that permits the date to be determined accurately throughout the year. (© Clive Ruggles)**

●

Adapted by Peigín Doyle from the conference presentation by Professor Clive Ruggles.

DARK SKY RESERVES

A dark night sky blazing with myriads of stars was part of the nightly human experience until very recent times, when artificial light started to lighten the night sky and blot out the starscape for the majority of the world's population.

The International Dark-Sky Association has initiated a programme to list and preserve the world's dark skies for their scientific, natural, educational, cultural, heritage and public enjoyment.

Designated dark sky reserves have an exceptional quality of starry nights and night environment. There are now over **100** listed Dark Sky sites around the world.

www.darksky.org/ (International Dark Sky Association)

STAR NAMING

Most star names derive from the Greek, Arabic and Chinese traditions. The International Astronomical Union has begun a process of finding cultural names for stars that haven't yet got internationally agreed names, with the aim of representing as broad a range of human cultures, past and present, as possible.

www.iau.org/public/themes/naming_stars/

'There is no more special place to be than on top of Loughcrew Carnbane East waiting for dawn when skies are clear. Below us the fog rolls in peaks like a gigantic ocean. It is as if we are on a hilltop island way above the world.'

'We spend most of the time inside asking people to get out of the way of the light. In their excited and distracted state, they stand still and lift their legs up as if the light were somehow a liquid, a puddle that they can step out of.'

'At Dowth, though, the light seems almost secondary to the sense of gathering and the excitement of being there.'

'No matter how often we tell those waiting that the light will hit the floor, they look longingly out towards the entrance. I sometimes think it is as if they are looking into the projector rather than at the screen.'

Clare Tuffy, Office of Public Works Ireland.

GLOSSARY

BEAKER POTTERY Beaker pottery is associated with the Beaker tradition that spread through much of western and central Europe in the European Early Bronze Age. The pottery vessels are flat-bottomed and shaped like an inverted bell or have a flared upper section. Beaker artefacts and cultural practices show great variation in different regions of Europe. Beaker vessels in Ireland were primarily used for domestic purposes rather than as grave-goods.

CARINATED BOWLS Carinated Bowls are an Early Neolithic style of pottery, found throughout Europe and Ireland, in which the neck or rim of the pot shows a sharp angle or the rim is 'rolled over' or flared.

CARROWKEEL WARE Carrowkeel Ware is a coarse-textured pottery associated with the Carrowkeel passage tomb cluster in County Sligo. The vessels are usually round-bottomed bowls, decorated with a stab-and-drag technique and sometimes with loop motifs.

COSMOLOGY 'The philosophical study of the origin and nature of the universe; the branch of astronomy concerned with the evolution and structure of the universe; a particular account of the origin and structure of the universe' (*Collins English Dictionary, Complete and Unabridged*, New Edition).

COSMOS The world or universe considered as an ordered system.

COURT TOMB Court tombs are megalithic chamber tombs. They are often trapeze-shaped, with a long barrow and an unroofed curvilinear court usually located at the end of the barrow. The court gives access to a gallery divided by large stones into individual chambers that house the burials. The forecourt was probably used for rituals associated with the dead. Court tombs were built roughly between 3700 and 3570 BC.

CROMARTY-TYPE TOMB The Cromarty-type tomb is one of two main types of Neolithic chambered tomb found on the Orkney Islands. The burial chamber is reached via a low passage and is divided by upright stone slabs into separate stalls.

CROMLECH An archaic term for a megalithic tomb in which a very big capstone is supported by large upright stones.

CULTURAL ASTRONOMY Cultural astronomy is the academic study of how different cultures, ancient and modern, perceive and interpret astronomy and the heavenly bodies. It draws on social, physical and natural science disciplines and is divided into two main areas of study: archaeoastronomy, which is the study of the astronomic practices and beliefs of ancient cultures, and ethnoastronomy, which is concerned with those of indigenous cultures and draws on ethnographic and historical records.

CUPMARKS A cupmark is a very common motif in prehistoric rock art and is found among cultures on all continents. It takes the form of a shallow circular depression with related motifs pecked or cut into the surface of the rock. Cupmarks are found on natural rocks, sometimes incorporating features on the natural surface of the stone, and on built megalithic structures such as passage graves. They have been found in contexts that suggest that they date from the Palaeolithic onwards.

EQUINOX The mid-points between the winter and summer solstices are called the spring and autumn equinoxes. These are the times when the sun is directly above the equator and night and day are of equal length in both northern and southern hemispheres.

FOOD VESSEL Food Vessel is the name given to a style of Early Bronze Age decorated pottery found in Britain and Ireland. In Ireland Food Vessel pots may have overlapped with the end of the Beaker tradition. They were used as grave-goods more often than Beaker pots, which were used for this purpose elsewhere.

GENESIS, BIBLE Genesis is the first book of the Hebrew Bible and of the Old Testament of the Christian Bible. It describes the creation of the world, humanity's relationship with God and the history of the Jewish people as God's chosen people.

HENGE A roughly circular or oval enclosure where an internal area is encircled by an earthen bank, with one or two openings, and ranging in size up to over 100m in diameter. Structural variations in different countries include an internal space defined by an inner ditch, a ring of timber or a water-filled circle. Henges often form a focal point in the landscape and were linked to ritual activity and communal gatherings over many millennia, in the case of Ireland extending from the Middle Neolithic to the Early Iron Age and beyond.

LINKARDSTOWN-TYPE TOMBS/ MOUNDS The Linkardstown type is a Neolithic tomb in which a box-shaped cist built of large slabs is found in the centre of a circular mound. It was inaccessible once covered by the mound, which consists of a stone core covered with sods and earth. Such tombs usually hold the remains of one person or a small number of people, usually male. They may be a regional development and are found mainly in the southern part of Ireland.

MAESHOWE-TYPE PASSAGE TOMBS
The Maeshowe type is the second of two main types of chambered tomb found in the Orkney Islands. The burial chamber is cruciform in layout and is reached via a long passage.

MOUND OF THE HOSTAGES, TARA
The Mound of the Hostages is a cairn- and earth-covered Neolithic passage tomb located on the Hill of Tara in County Meath. Analysis of its earliest burials found them to date from *c.* 3350–3100 cal. BC. Burials and artefacts from the Bronze Age and later periods were incorporated into the original tomb.

NAZCA GEOGLYPHS A geoglyph is a large design on the ground made of rock fragments, stone, gravel or earth. They are created either by arranging rock materials on the ground in the desired shape or by removing them to expose finer ground below. The Nazca people settled in the Nazca and adjacent valleys of southern coastal Peru between *c.* 200 BC and AD 600. Their culture is noted for its ornate pottery and textiles and particularly for the distinctive geoglyphs that they created on the desert floor. Sometimes called 'Nazca lines', they are huge stylised images of animals, plants and humans or straight or curved lines. Theories of their meaning abound but they are believed to have been related to religious activities and also to the Nazca preoccupation with water.

PASSAGE TOMB A passage tomb consists of a circular mound, in Ireland ringed with a kerb of large stones, within which is a stone passageway leading to a large internal burial chamber containing mostly cremated human remains. It is roofed by lintels or by overlapping corbelled slabs and may be covered with sods or earth.

PORTAL TOMB Portal tombs were built with two high portal stones at the front and a lower back stone; these carry a very large roof stone whose heaviest end sits above the tomb entrance. Side slabs form the sides of the chamber and another upright slab between the portal stones closes the entrance. The evidence from Poulnabrone suggests that portal tombs were built between 3800 and 3200 BC and there is evidence of repeated inhumed burials. The 191 known Irish portal tombs are found in the northern half of the country, in the region between Dublin and Waterford and in Clare–south Galway.

RING-CAIRN A ring-cairn is a low bank of earth and stones surrounding an open, circular area of ground. The bank is sometimes rimmed by larger stones. The central area is empty, though on some sites burials or cremated remains have been found. Ring-cairns date from the Bronze Age.

RING-DITCH This is a circular earthwork with or without an opening. Ditches dug at the base of circular houses or barrows are technically ring-ditches, but in Ireland the term is normally reserved for self-contained ditches associated with burial and other ritual activity. A ring-ditch comprises a roughly circular trench cut into the soil and sometimes into the underlying bedrock. Human bone may occur in the ditch or in the enclosed area. Variations are found in many countries and cultures, often dating from the Neolithic and the Bronze Age. Some ring-ditches in Ireland date from the Iron Age.

RINGFORT The ringfort is a circular enclosed settlement or farmstead dating mainly from the early medieval period in Ireland, *c.* AD 600–900, and occasionally up to the arrival of the Anglo-Normans in the twelfth century. The habitations were enclosed by one or more earthen banks and/or a timber palisade. Smaller enclosures may have been used as animal pens. Ringforts varied in size and in the number of enclosing banks, which indicated the social status or role of the main occupant.

SOLSTICE In both northern and southern parts of the earth, the solstice is the day when there are most or least hours of sunlight. Viewed from the northern hemisphere, the longest day, with most daylight hours, is the summer solstice on 21 June. The day of fewest sunlight hours, or the longest night, is 21 December. The sun stops at its most northerly point in the sky on the summer solstice, giving most daylight, or at its most southerly limit at the winter solstice. These two days are dated according to the Gregorian calendar, but in practice the phenomenon can vary from the calendar date, as the sun seems to stand still on the horizon for a few days on either side of the 21st. This happens because the earth's axis is tilted and its orbit around the sun is elliptical rather than circular.

UNSTAN WARE Unstan Ware is one of two styles of Neolithic pottery found on Orkney. It is round-bottomed and is decorated with grooved patterning around the rim. It is associated with the Early Neolithic on Orkney.

WEDGE TOMB This is a wedge- or U-shaped cairn covering a long burial gallery, which is higher and wider near the entrance and drops in height towards the back. The large roof stones are supported by tall side stones. At the western end is an antechamber separated by upright slabs from the main burial chamber. The entrance is aligned on the west or south-west, the direction of the setting sun. In Ireland wedge tombs date from the very Late Neolithic to the Early Bronze Age.

BIOGRAPHIES

Writer

PEIGÍN DOYLE is a writer, editor and journalist who has had a lifelong curiosity about the history and heritage of place and how the world might have looked through our ancestors' eyes. She has written on many aspects of archaeology and heritage.

Contributors

The prehistoric sky, 3000 BC to 500 BC. Chapter 4

RICHARD BRADLEY is Emeritus Professor at Reading University. His research on the prehistory of western and northern Europe includes landscape archaeology, monumental architecture, rock art and hoards.

A cosmological interpretation of the alignments of Neolithic burial monuments in Orkney. Chapter 3

JANE DOWNES is Director of the University of the Highlands and Islands Archaeology Institute, Orkney, Scotland, and has researched extensively on prehistoric burial monuments and domestic architecture. She is part of the Heart of Neolithic Orkney World Heritage Site Steering Group, developed the Research Agenda and Strategy for the Orkney World Heritage Site and contributed to the Brú na Bóinne WHS Research Framework.

Winter solstice at Knockroe, County Kilkenny. Chapter 6

MUIRIS O'SULLIVAN has published extensively on passage tombs and megalithic art; he is the author of *Duma na nGiall* (2005) and lead editor of *Tara—from the past to the future* (2013), both published by Wordwell. He directed five seasons of archaeological excavation at Knockroe passage tomb, a project now nearing publication. He is a member of the Heritage Council and a former head of the UCD School of Archaeology.

Skyscape, culture and the Irish passage tomb tradition: a complex legacy. Chapter 5

FRANK PRENDERGAST is Emeritus at the Technological University Dublin, where he researches Irish prehistoric monuments and their landscapes from a cultural astronomy perspective. His current interests and publications are on the meaning of the dark sky in the prehistoric past and on the conservation of archaeological landscapes from light pollution.

Cultural astronomy and cultural heritage: a global perspective. Chapter 8

CLIVE RUGGLES is Emeritus Professor of

Archaeoastronomy in the School of Archaeology and Ancient History at the University of Leicester. His early work on Scotland and Ireland, culminated in his award-winning book Astronomy in prehistoric Britain and Ireland, (Yale 1999). Over his career, he has written numerous books, papers and articles on subjects ranging from prehistoric Europe and pre-Columbian America to indigenous astronomies in Africa.

Sunrise orientations and the European megalithic phenomenon. Chapter 1

CHRIS SCARRE is Professor of Archaeology

at Durham University and a specialist in the later prehistory of Atlantic Europe (Portugal, France, Britain and Ireland), with a particular focus on monumentality and landscape.

Through a glass darkly: orientation uncertainty, passages and stars in the western Iberian tradition. Chapter 2

FABIO SILVA is a Lecturer in Archaeological

Modelling at the Department of Archaeology and Anthropology of Bournemouth University, and co-founder and co-editor of the *Journal of Skyscape*

Archaeology. His research interests are on how societies have perceived and conceived their environment and used that knowledge to time and adjust social, productive and magico-religious behaviours..

CLARE TUFFY has worked in the Boyne

Valley for the Office of Public Works for nearly 40 years. She is Visitor Services Manager at the Brú na Bóinne Centre, Co. Meath.

Art, architecture and astronomy in the Irish passage tomb tradition. Chapter 7

KEN WILLIAMS is a photographer and

researcher specializing in the prehistoric art and monuments of western Europe. His photographic project 'Shadows and Stone' featured as a cover story in the *Irish Times* magazine. His work and pioneering use of photographic and lighting techniques have featured in a large number of academic and popular publications nationally and internationally.

REFERENCES

UNESCO, 2016, www.whc.unesco.org/en/astronomy/.

UNESCO, 2018, www.whc.unesco.org/en/news/1830.

UNESCO, 2010, www.whc.unesco.org/en/religious-sacred-heritage/.

Gatton, M., 2010. *The Camera Obscura and the Megalithic Tomb: The role of projected solar images in the symbolic renewal of Life.* http://paleo-camera.com/neolithic/)

O'Sullivan, M., 2005. *Duma na nGiall: Tara The Mound of the Hostages.* Dublin: Wordwell.

Prendergast, F., 2018. *Solar Alignment and the Irish passage tomb tradition.* Heritage Guide 82. Dublin: *Archaeology Ireland*.

O'Sullivan, M. (lead ed), Doyle, M. and Scarre, C. (eds). 2013. *Tara–From the past to the future.* Dublin: Wordwell with UCD School of Archaeology.

Prendergast, F., O'Sullivan, M., Williams, K. and Cooney, G., 2017. Facing the Sun. *Archaeology Ireland* 122: 10-17.

Rappaport, R.A., 1999. *Ritual and religion in the making of humanity.* Cambridge: Cambridge University Press.

Ross, J. and Davidson, I., 2006. Rock art and ritual: an archaeological analysis of rock art in arid central Australia. *Journal of Archaeological Method and Theory* 13, 305-41.

Ruggles, C., 1999. *Astronomy in prehistoric Britain and Ireland.* London and New Haven: Yale University Press.

Ballin Smith, B., 2014, *Crantit subterranean chambered tomb, St Ola, Orkney.* UK: Orcadian.

UNESCO, 2010. *Initiative on Heritage of Religious Interest.* [online].

UNESCO, 2016. *Astronomy and World Heritage Thematic Initiative.* [online].

UNESCO, 2018. *Gran Canaria Recommendation* (from International Expert Meeting on Astronomical Heritage and Sacred Places, May 2018) [online].

Watson, A. and Scott, R., 2016. "Materialising Light, Making Worlds: Optical Image Projection within the Megalithic Passage Tombs of Britain and Ireland." In *The Oxford Handbook of Light in Archaeology,* edited by Papadopolos, C. and Graeme, E. Oxford: Oxford University Press.

Whitley, D. S., 2014. Hunter-gatherer Religion and Ritual. In *The Oxford Handbook of the Archaeology and Anthropology of Hunter-gatherers,* edited by V. Cummings, P. Jordan and M. Zvelebil, 1221-42. Oxford: Oxford University Press.

Williams, K., 2019. Rekindling the solstice light. *Archaeology Ireland* 130, 19-24.